The Plutarch Project

Volume Ten

Phocion, Camillus, and Dion

by

Anne E. White

Cover photograph and cover design: Bryan White

ISBN: 978-1-7772522-6-7

CONTENTS

Introduction i

Phocion 1

- Lesson One 4
- Lesson Two 8
- Lesson Three 12
- Lesson Four 16
- Lesson Five 21
- Lesson Six 26
- Lesson Seven 30
- Lesson Eight 35
- Lesson Nine 39
- Lesson Ten 44
- Lesson Eleven 50
- Lesson Twelve and Examination Questions 55

Marcus Furius Camillus 59

- Lesson One 63
- Lesson Two 69
- Lesson Three 73
- Lesson Four 78
- Lesson Five 83
- Lesson Six 87

Lesson Seven 92
Lesson Eight 97
Lesson Nine 101
Lesson Ten 106
Lesson Eleven 109
Lesson Twelve and Examination Questions 115
Dion of Syracuse 121
Lesson One 125
Lesson Two 130
Lesson Three 134
Lesson Four 139
Lesson Five 145
Lesson Six 149
Lesson Seven 154
Lesson Eight 159
Lesson Nine 163
Lesson Ten 168
Lesson Eleven 174
Lesson Twelve and Examination Questions 180
Bibliography 187

Introduction

These notes, and the accompanying text, are prepared for the use of individual students and small groups following a twelve-week term.

The text is a free mixture of Thomas North's 1579 translation of Plutarch's *Lives of the Noble Greeks and Romans* and John Dryden's 1683 translation. (Dryden for clarity, North for character.) Omissions have been made for length and suitability for the intended age group.

Those using audio versions or other translations may want to preview those editions for similar "necessary omissions."

Using the Lesson Material

> "We do not tell the tales, we know we cannot, we read them as well as we know how and without comment, unless questions are asked. We rely upon the imagination of the children to work upon this material until it becomes theirs, and I think we do not deceive ourselves by so doing." (E.A. Parish in *The Parents' Review*)

Each study contains explanatory material before the first lesson. A little at the beginning may be useful to stir interest in the study, but it is not meant to be given all in one dose! I encourage you to make the lessons your own. Use the questions that are the most meaningful to you.

Some lessons are divided into two or three sections. These can be read all at once or used throughout the week.

Examination Questions

The three studies include questions for end-of-term examinations, which have been written especially for this volume.

Phocion

(c. 402-318 B.C.)

"…Demosthenes indeed was a great orator, but Phocion's tongue had a sharper understanding, because in few words, he comprehended much matter. And to this purpose, they say that Demosthenes himself said also, that as oft as he saw Phocion get up into the pulpit for orations to speak against him, he was wont to say to his friends: 'See, the axe of my words riseth.' And yet it is hard to judge, whether he spake that in respect of his tongue, or rather for the estimation he had gotten, because of his great wisdom…" (Plutarch, *Life of Demosthenes*)

Who was Phocion?

Phocion borrowed a life motto from the goddess Athena: "Skillful to rule in war and peace." As a young man, he became respected both for his skill in speaking and his bravery in battle. Although he was not a promoter of war, he never backed down from what had to be done.

However, he was also known for a number of personal quirks, some of them relating to his schooling in **Stoic** philosophy. **Stoicism** taught that it was better to ignore unimportant matters such as pleasure or pain, so that one could face any situation honestly and calmly. Those who have read Plutarch's *Life of Cato the Younger* will recognize similarities, as Cato followed the later Roman revival of Stoicism.

The World of Phocion

The Athens in which Phocion grew up was a very different place than it had been during the "golden" years of Pericles. After being defeated by Sparta in the Peloponnesian Wars, the state was in political and economic trouble. In Phocion's adult years, an even greater threat was the increasing power of Macedon.

Is it Macedon or Macedonia? Were the Macedonians Greeks?

The names are used interchangeably. Macedonia, or Macedon, was a kingdom in the northeastern part of mainland Greece. The Macedonians were Greek in many respects, such as religious beliefs; but they valued their distinct heritage and identity.

For many years, the dominant political power in Europe and the Middle East had been the Persian empire; but Persia's strength had weakened, and its subjects were becoming rebellious. Philip II of Macedon planned to combine Macedon's military power with that of the Greek states, and thus to attack Persia; but his death in 336 B.C. left that ambition unfulfilled. However, his son Alexander spent the next thirteen years conquering not only Persia, but a previously undreamed-of share of the world.

Who was Antipater?

(Pronounced An-TIP-a-ter) Antipater was a Macedonian general under Philip II and then under Alexander the Great. He was an advisor and friend to Alexander during the early years of his reign, and he acted as regent (substitute ruler) when Alexander was in Persia and India. After Alexander's death, he became the self-declared (though short-lived) regent over the empire.

Who was Demosthenes?

Demosthenes was an orator, a philosopher, a public prosecutor and defender, and a political analyst. He was known for his strong anti-Macedonian views.

Who was Demades?

Demades, another Athenian orator, supported Demosthenes' views at first, but later they became enemies because of their differing ideas. Demades was taken prisoner at the Battle of Chaeronea (**Lesson Five**), but made such a good impression on King Philip that he was released. He also helped create a peace treaty between Macedon and Athens, but he was disgraced over the Harpalus scandal (**Lesson Seven**). In the post-Philip-and-Alexander era, Demades enjoyed a period of successful leadership; but his tendency to act in his own best interests eventually led to his death.

Top Vocabulary Terms

If you know these words, you're well on your way to mastering the vocabulary for the *Life of Phocion*. These terms will not be repeated in the lessons.

1. **austere:** stern; cold-looking; without any decoration

2. **commonwealth:** a country or city/state (like Athens), and its colonies or associated territories or countries.

3. **galley:** a ship which was powered mainly by banks of oars

4. **imperious:** arrogant, domineering

5. **importune:** pester; bother someone. To be **importunate** is to be annoyingly persistent.

6. **oligarchy:** government or leadership made up of a small, elite

group, as opposed to **democracy** (a form of government in which many people have a vote). The actual word does not appear in the story, but it is worth knowing, as Phocion's eventual downfall was caused by his support of **oligarchy**.

7. **orator:** a public speaker. The orators of Athens made speeches and also debated legal and political issues, so their ideas carried weight in the **commonwealth**.

8. **tractable:** easy to deal with or to control. Intractable, on the other hand, means hard to control.

9. **tyrant:** The idea of a "tyrant" in the ancient world was somewhat different from the way we use the word "tyrant" today. It meant an absolute ruler, but it wasn't a judgment about whether he was good or evil.

10. **victuals:** (pronounced "vittles") food supplies

Lesson One

Introduction

In this introductory lesson, we are given glimpses of Phocion as a young student of philosophy, and as an older man who was mocked for his lack of sociability and for his extreme simplicity in dress. Those who saw behind those eccentricities described a "powerful speaker" and someone "full of wisdom," with a talent for getting to the point.

Vocabulary

in the interest of Antipater…: this will be explained later

government: leadership

dissolutely: with no moral restraint

calamities: disasters

school of Academia: the school (or Academy) founded by Plato

in the camp: when on a military campaign

bending of his brows: Dryden: "his frowning looks"

maxims: proverbs, wise sayings

intrinsic: natural, essential

cutter: or "axe"

People

Demades, **Antipater**, **Demosthenes:** see introductory notes

Plato: a famous philosopher of ancient Athens

Xenocrates: a philosopher who believed that virtue produces happiness

Chares: Athenian politician and military commander

Zeno: Zeno of Elea, the philosopher who founded **Stoicism**

Historic Occasions

402 B.C.: Birth of Phocion

400 B.C.: Birth of Antipater

384 B.C.: Birth of Demosthenes

382 B.C.: Birth of Philip (who became Philip II of Macedon)

380 B.C.: Birth of Demades

On the Map

As an introduction to this *Life*, it would be useful to look at maps of ancient **Greece**. Look for **Athens**, in the region of **Attica**; **Sparta**, in the **Peloponnesus** (the southern part of Greece); and the **Isthmus of Corinth**, which divides the country almost in two. It would be good to point out the island of **Euboea**, and the region of **Boeotia**.

Phocion's colleagues suggested that he needed to "lighten up." What was his response?

Creative narration #1: When Phocion was about fifteen, the philosopher Plato founded the famous Academy in Athens. We know that Phocion studied there at some point, and that he developed long-lasting friendships (**Lesson Four**). Imagine a conversation between young Phocion and his parents or friends, describing his interest in attending this new school.

Creative narration #2: Phocion's speeches "crowded the greatest amount of significance into the smallest allowance of space." Choose a topic to write or speak on. Then cut the word allowance or the time limit in half (or quarters), and see if you can say more with less.

Lesson Two

Introduction

In this lesson we see Phocion moving into his adult responsibilities as a military leader and a civil administrator. Since he himself seemed able to handle both roles, he saw no reason why those parts of Athenian life should have to function separately, and he campaigned for a more streamlined relationship (or more overlap) between the two.

Vocabulary

the wars: the Theban-Spartan War (see **Historic Occasions**)

Feast Day of the Great Mysteries: the Eleusinian Mysteries were religious initiation ceremonies held twice yearly

Boedromion: the Greek month equal to September/October

tribute: a tax, or something owed (often to a ruler)

impertinent: rude

like so much land…: as if the government were divided up like garden plots

Pallas: another name for Athena, the patron goddess of Athens

shunning or declining: refusing to take on responsibility

People

Captain Chabrias: described by Demosthenes as one of the most successful naval commanders in Athenian history

Ctesippus: pronounced something like "Te-SIB-is"

Eubulus: Athenian politician, noted for his skill in finance

Aristophon (of Azenia); Lycurgus (of Athens); Hypereides: Athenian orators

Diopeithes: an Athenian general

Leosthenes (#1): either the Athenian admiral who was exiled after a failed battle in 361 B.C.; or the same person as **Leosthenes (#2)**, a commander in the Lamian Wars who first appears in **Lesson Seven**.

Chares: the naval commander who replaced **Leosthenes (#1)**

Pericles, Aristides, and Solon: great Athenian leaders of the past

Historic Occasions

395-387 B.C.: Corinthian War

378-362 B.C.: Theban-Spartan War, also called the Boeotian War

376 B.C.: Athens defeated Sparta at the Battle of Naxos

357-355 B.C.: The Social War (Four of Athens' allies wanted to break away from the league, but Athens was not willing to let them go.)

357 B.C.: Death of Chabrias at Chios

of his own times, but of those preceding him; never, indeed, promoting or encouraging military expeditions, yet never on the other hand, **shunning or declining** when he was called upon by the public voice.

Narration and Discussion

How was the friendship between Phocion and Chabrias beneficial for both of them?

For older students and further thought: Athens is often praised as the birthplace of democracy. However, Phocion, as a student of Plato, saw weaknesses in a system where just "anyone" could run for office or have an equal vote. What are the advantages and disadvantages of **democracy** and **oligarchy**? Are there alternatives?

Creative narration: Write or act out the scene between Phocion and Ctesippus.

Lesson Three

Introduction

Rather than continuing with historical events, Plutarch spends extra time here building our understanding of Phocion's character.

Vocabulary

general: An Athenian public office much like the Roman consul; those elected were responsible for both military and civic affairs.

upon slight occasions: at times of little importance

spruce: pleasing in appearance; tidy, clean

oracle from Delphi: The temple at Delphi was believed to be a place where divine messages were received.

"Alas, hath not some evil thing…": "What did I say wrong?"

peremptorily: in a way that leaves no room for argument

churlishly: rudely; in this context, in an unfriendly manner

timorous: fearful, timid

bounds and frontiers: the boundaries between their territories

surname of "Good": A surname, in the ancient world, was an extra name given to show someone's character, or to honour a particular event such as a battle victory. Phocion's surname, *Chrēstos*, meant "Benefactor," or "Do-good."

hostility: opposition, unfriendliness

contend: argue, fight

adversary: opponent; one taking the opposite side of an issue

espouse: support; adopt, take on something (like a cause)

patronage: support

indifferent: questionable; not very good

sent to prison: Aristogeiton's father died in prison because of a debt he owed the state, and his son inherited the debt.

On the Map

Boeotia (Boeotians): a region which included the city of **Thebes**

Reading

Part One

Phocion was no less than forty-five times chosen **general**; he being never on any one of those occasions present at the election, but having the command, in his absence, conferred on him. Insomuch that it amazed those who did not well consider to see the people always prefer Phocion, who was so far from honouring them or courting their favour, that he always thwarted and opposed them. But so it was: as great men and princes are said to call in their flatterers when dinner has been served, so the Athenians, **upon slight occasions**, entertained and diverted themselves with their **"spruce"** speakers and trim orators; but when it came to action, they were sober and considerate enough to single out the most austere and wisest for public employment, however he might be opposed to their wishes and sentiments.

For once an **oracle from Delphi** was openly read before them, which said that, all the other Athenians being agreed, yet there was one among them that was contrary to all the rest of the city. Phocion, stepping forth before them all, bade them never seek further for the man, for it was he that liked none of all their doings. Another time he chanced to say his opinion before all the people, the which they all praised and approved: but he saw they were so suddenly become of his mind, he turned back to his friends, and asked them, **"Alas, hath not some evil thing slipped my mouth unawares?"**

Upon occasion of a public festivity, being solicited for his financial contribution by the example of others, and the people pressing him much, he bade them apply themselves to the wealthy; for his part, he said, he should blush to make a present *here*, rather than a repayment *there*, turning and pointing to Callicles, the money-lender. Being still clamoured upon and importuned, he told them this tale:

> "A certain cowardly fellow setting out for the wars, hearing the ravens croak in his passage, threw down his arms, resolving to wait. Presently he took them and ventured out again, but hearing the same music, once more made a stop. 'For,' said he, 'you may croak till you are tired, but you shall make no dinner upon me.'"

Part Two

The Athenians urging him at an unseasonable time to lead them out against the enemy, he **peremptorily** refused: thereupon they called him a coward. "Well," said he again, "it is not you can make me valiant, no more than myself can make you cowards; and yet we know one another."

Another time in a marvellous dangerous time, the people handled him very **churlishly**, demanding a strict account of how the public money had been employed, and the like: but he answered them, "First, good friends, make sure you are safe." After a war, during which they had been very tractable and **timorous**, when, upon peace being made, they began again to be confident and overbearing, and to cry out upon Phocion as having lost them the honour of victory. To all their clamour he made only this answer: "You are happy that have a captain that knows you, else you would sing a new song."

Another time there was a quarrel betwixt the **Boeotians** and the Athenians, about their **bounds and frontiers**: the which they would not try by law, but by battle. But Phocion counselled them rather to fight it out in words, in which they were the stronger, and not with weapons, where they were the weaker.

Another time they so much misliked his opinion in the assembly, that they would not abide to hear him, nor suffer him to speak. "Well, my masters," quoth he then, "you may make me do that which is not to be done: but you shall never compel me, against my mind, to say that which is not to be spoken." Among the many public speakers who opposed him, Demosthenes, for example, once told him, "The Athenians, Phocion, will kill you some day when they are in a rage." "And you," said he, "if they once are in their senses."

[omission for length and content]

Part Three

So that oftentimes it makes me muse, how, or wherefore so sharp and severe a man (as by these examples it appeareth he was) could come to the **surname of "Good."** Notwithstanding, in the end I find it a hard thing, but not impossible, that a man should be like wine, both sweet and sharp together: as there are others to the contrary, that at the first sight, seem very courteous and gentle of conversation, and upon better acquaintance, prove churlish and dogged.

[omission for length]

Phocion never allowed himself from any feeling of personal **hostility** to do hurt to any fellow-citizen; nor, indeed, reputed any man his enemy, except so far as he could not but **contend** sharply with such as opposed the measures he urged for the public good; in which argument he was, indeed, a rude, obstinate, and uncompromising **adversary**. For his general conversation, it was easy, courteous, and obliging to all, to the point that he would befriend his very opponents in their distress, and **espouse** the cause of those who differed most from him, when they needed his **patronage**. His friends, reproaching him for pleading on behalf of a man of **indifferent** character, he told them the innocent had no need of an advocate. A troublesome orator, Aristogeiton (one whom Phocion had previously called "worthless") was **sent to prison**, and sent earnestly to Phocion to speak with him there; but his friends dissuaded him from going. "Nay, by your favour," said he, "where should I rather choose to pay Aristogeiton a visit?"

Narration and Discussion

What things about Phocion's character were the most puzzling to the people around him?

For older students: "You may make me do that which is not to be done: but you shall never compel me, against my mind, to say that which is not to be spoken." Dryden translates this as "You may compel me to act against my wishes, but you shall never force me to speak against my judgment." Is that a good personal rule?

Creative narration: If you are working with a group, have one person play the part of an Athenian reporter assigned to do a story about Phocion, and ask others to tell the stories they have heard about him (these can be drawn from any of the first three lessons); why Phocion always gets elected, even though he doesn't show up for the elections; and/or why he earned the nickname "Phocion the Good."

Lesson Four

Introduction

Increased aggression from Macedon now began to divide the Greek city-states. Some cities, like Chalcis, saw no point in holding out, and capitulated to Philip's invading forces. Others, like Eretrea, called on allies such as Athens for assistance. Athens, having lost its earlier glory as head of the Greek empire, was limited in its ability to help; but Phocion did his best to lead the Athenians in supporting their friends and discouraging Philip, at least for the time being.

Vocabulary

imminent: about to happen

deferred: put off, postponed

dispersed: scattered

footmen: foot soldiers; infantry

signal: great, significant

the means placed in his hands: what he was given to work with

chafed: annoyed

requite: repay, return

to boot: as well

People

Plutarch of Eretria: or Plutarchus; a tyrant ruler who asked Athens for help when a neighbouring ruler, **Callias of Chalcis**, formed an alliance with Macedon and threatened to attack Eretria

Chares: See **Lesson One.**

Historic Occasions

359 B.C.: Philip became king of Macedon

356 B.C.: Birth of Alexander the Great (son of Philip)

c. 355 B.C.: Birth of Antipater's son Cassander

and rally those who came in from the previous flight. He himself, with a body of his best men, gave charge upon the enemies.

The fight was cruel between them. For the Athenians fought very valiantly, with **signal** courage and gallantry. Thallus, the son of Cineas, and Glaucus of Polymedes, who fought near the general, gained the honours of the day. And so did Cleophanes that day also shew himself very valiant. For he, crying out still upon the horsemen that fled, and persuading them to come and help their general that was in danger, brought them back again, and thereby got the footmen the victory.

Phocion now expelled Plutarch from Eretria, and possessed himself of the very important fort of **Zaretra**, situated where the island is pinched in, as it were, by the seas on each side, and its breadth most reduced to a narrow girth. He released all the Greeks whom he took, out of fear of the orators at Athens, thinking they might very likely persuade the people in their anger into committing some act of cruelty.

After all these things were done, Phocion returned back to Athens. But then did the confederates of the Athenians straight away wish for his justice and courtesy, as the Athenians that of his experience and courage. For his successor Molossus, that was general for the rest of the war, had no better success than to fall alive into the enemy's hands.

Part Two

Then King Philip, being put in marvellous great hope, went with all his army into **the Hellespont**, persuading himself that he should straight take all the **Chersonesus**, the cities of **Perinthus** and **Byzantium**. The Athenians raised a force to relieve them, but the popular leaders proposed **Chares** to be general; who, sailing thither, effected nothing worthy of **the means placed in his hands**. The cities were afraid, and would not receive his ships into their harbours, so that he did nothing but wander about, raising money from their friends, and despised by their enemies. When the Athenians, **chafed** by the orators, were extremely indignant, and repented having ever sent any help to the Byzantines, Phocion rose and told them they ought not to be angry with the allies for distrusting, but with their generals that deserved to be mistrusted. "For they," said he, "do make your confederates afraid of you, who without you notwithstanding cannot save themselves."

The people, changing their minds by his oration, made Phocion again their captain, and sent him with an army into the Hellespont to help their confederates there: an appointment which, in effect, contributed more than anything to the relief of Byzantium. For Phocion's name was already honourably known; and an old acquaintance of his, who had been his fellow-student in the Academy, Leon, a man of high renown for virtue among the Byzantines, having vouched for Phocion to the city, they opened their gates to receive him; not permitting him, though he desired it, to encamp outside the walls, but entertained him and all the Athenians with perfect reliance; while they, to **requite** their confidence, behaved among their new hosts soberly and inoffensively, and exerted themselves on all occasions with the greatest zeal and resolution for their defense.

Thus King Philip, whom, till now, it had been thought impossible to match, or even to oppose, was driven out of the Hellespont, and was despised **to boot**. Phocion also took some of his ships, and recaptured some of the places he had garrisoned, making besides several inroads into the country, which he plundered and overran, until he received a wound from some of the enemy who came to the defense, and, thereupon, sailed away home.

Narration and Discussion

Explain how Phocion helped the Athenians win against Philip at Eretrea, and then found a way to end the siege of Byzantium. What made him successful in these battles, especially when others had failed?

Creative narration: Write or act out a conversation between Phocion and his old friend Leon.

Lesson Five

Introduction

Athens now found its own existence threatened by the growing Macedonian power. Phocion, recognizing the strength of the enemy, recommended that Athens accept Philip's terms of surrender; but he was outvoted, and the Athenians were massacred at the ensuing battle.

Then, in a strange turn of events, the Athenians received the news that Philip had been killed by one of his own bodyguards. In the months that followed, Greek cities such as Thebes and Athens struggled against Macedonian control. The new king Alexander retaliated by destroying Thebes, and he demanded that the Athenians surrender their rebellious orators, especially Demosthenes (who had made himself extremely unpopular with both Philip and Alexander). However, Alexander agreed to reconsider his decree; and he also seemed interested in Phocion's helpful suggestion that he should go and attack the Persians instead.

Vocabulary

deliver their city into his hands: they were not surrendering to Athens, but rather asking for its help against Macedon

arsenal: place where weapons and ammunition are stored

clamourers and incendiaries: those who liked to stir things up

council of the Areopagus: the high council of the city

the common treaty of peace: a general Greek peace treaty

concurrence: agreement

affright: fear

barbarians: refers specifically to the Persians

People

Charidemus: Although Charidemus was from Euboea, he had often led the Athenian troops against Philip.

Alexander: Alexander the Great (see introductory notes)

Historic Occasions

338 B.C.: Athens defeated at Chaeronea

336 B.C.: Death of Philip II of Macedon; accession of Alexander III

335 B.C.: After a Theban-Athenian rebellion against Macedon, Alexander destroyed Thebes.

334 B.C.: Alexander began his invasion of the Persian empire

On the Map

Megara (Megarians): a city in the western part of Attica

Nisaea: the Megarian harbour town

Reading

Part One

Shortly after, the **Megarians** secretly sent unto him to **deliver their city into his hands**. Phocion, fearing lest the Boeotians should hear of it and that they would prevent him: he called a common assembly early in the morning, and told the people what message the Megarians had sent unto him. The people upon his motion were determined to aid them; and Phocion, straight sounding the trumpet at the breaking up of the assembly, gave them no further leisure, but to take their weapons, and so led them immediately to **Megara**. The Megarians received them joyfully, and he proceeded to fortify **Nisaea**, and built two new long walls from the city to the **arsenal**, and so joined it to the sea: so that having now little reason to regard the enemies on the land side, it placed its dependence entirely on the Athenians.

Part Two

Now when the Athenians had proclaimed open war against King Philip, and had chosen other captains in Phocion's absence: he, on his arrival from the islands, tried to persuade the Athenians, that *[omission]* they should consent to a treaty. He was contradicted in this by one of the regular frequenters of the courts of justice, a common accuser, who said unto him: "Why, Phocion, how darest thou attempt to turn the Athenians from war, having now their swords in their hands?" "Yes, truly," said Phocion, "though in war I know I shall command thee, and in peace thou wilt command me."

But the people would not hearken to him, and Demosthenes carried them away with his persuasions, who counselled them to fight with King Philip, as far from Attica as they could. "Good friends," then said Phocion, "let us not dispute *where* we shall fight, but consider *how* we shall overcome. That will be the way to keep it at a distance. If we are beaten, it will be quickly at our doors."

[*At the Battle of Chaeronea, the armies of Athens and Thebes were destroyed, and the Greeks were now under the rule of Macedon.*]

Part Three

After the defeat, the **clamourers and incendiaries** in the town proposed **Charidemus** to be chosen general of the Athenians. The best of the citizens were in a panic, and supporting themselves with the aid of the **council of the Areopagus**, with entreaties and tears, they prevailed upon the people to have Phocion entrusted instead with the care of the city. He thought good to accept the articles and gentle conditions of peace which Philip offered them. But after that the orator Demades moved that the city of Athens would enter into **the common treaty of peace,** in **concurrence** with the rest of the states of Greece, Phocion would not agree to it, until they might understand what the particulars were which Philip demanded. He was overruled in this, under the pressure of the time; but almost immediately after, the Athenians repented it, when they understood that by these articles they were obliged to furnish Philip with both ships and horsemen.

"It was the fear of this," said Phocion, "that occasioned my opposition. But since the thing is done, let us make the best of it, and not be discouraged. Our forefathers were sometimes in command, and sometimes under it; and yet have so wisely and discreetly governed themselves in both fortunes, that they have not only saved their city, but all Greece besides."

Part Four

When news came of King Philip's death, the people for joy would straight have made bonfires and sacrifices to the gods for the good news; but Phocion would not suffer them, and said that "it was a token of a base mind to rejoice at any man's death; and besides that, the army which overthrew you at Chaeronea hath not yet lost but one man."

[omission for length]

After Thebes was lost, and **Alexander** had demanded Demosthenes, Lycurgus, Hypereides, and Caridemus to be delivered up: the whole assembly turning their eyes to him, and calling on Phocion by name to deliver his opinion, at last he rose up, and taking one of his friends unto him called Nicocles, whom he loved and trusted above all men else, he said thus openly unto them:

> "These men whom Alexander requireth have brought this city to this extremity, that if he required Nicocles here, I would give my consent to deliver him: for I would think myself happy to lose my life for all your safety. Furthermore, though I am right heartily sorry (said he) for the poor afflicted Thebans, that are come into the city for succour: yet I assure ye, it is better that one city mourn, than two. And therefore I think it best to entreat the Conqueror for both, rather than to our certain destruction to fight with him that is the stronger."

When this was decreed by the people, Alexander is said to have rejected their first address when it was presented, throwing it from him scornfully, and turning his back upon the ambassadors, who left him in **affright**. But the second, which Phocion himself brought, he took: being told by the older Macedonians that King Philip made great account of him. Whereupon, Alexander did not only give him audience, and grant his request, but further followed his counsel. For Phocion persuaded him that, if his designs were for quietness, he should make peace at once; if glory were his aim, he should make war not upon Greece, but on the **barbarians**.

So Phocion feeding Alexander's humour with such talk and discourse as he thought would like best, he so altered and softened Alexander's disposition that when he went from him, he (Alexander)

Athens, Phocion asked them that brought it why Alexander gave him such a great reward, above all the other citizens of Athens. "Because," said they, "he only esteemeth thee to be a good and honest man." Phocion replied again, "Then let him give me leave to be what I seem, and am, whilst I live." Following him to his house, and observing his simple and plain way of living, his wife employed in kneading bread with her own hands, himself drawing water to wash his feet, they pressed him to accept it, with some indignation, being ashamed, as they said, that Alexander's friend should live so miserably and beggarly as he did. Then Phocion, seeing a poor old man go by in a threadbare gown, asked them, whether they thought him worse than he? "No, God forbid," answered they again. Then replied he again, "He lives with less than I do, and yet is contented, and hath enough. To be short," said he, "if I should take this sum of money and use it not, it is as much as I had it not: on the other side, if I use it, I shall make all the city speak ill of the king and me both."

So this great present was sent back from Athens, whereby he showed the Grecians that he who needed not such gold and silver was richer than he that gave it to him. And when Alexander was displeased, and wrote back to him to say that he could not esteem those his friends who would not be **obliged by him**, not even would this induce Phocion to accept the money, but only requested him for his sake, that he would set four men at liberty which were kept prisoners in the city of Sardis, for certain accusations laid against them *[omission for length]*. This was instantly granted by Alexander, and they were set at liberty.

Afterwards, when sending Craterus into Macedon, Alexander commanded him to make Phocion an offer of four cities in Asia *[omission]*, any one of which, at his choice, should be delivered to him; insisting yet more positively with him, and declaring he (Alexander) should resent it, should he (Phocion) continue obstinate in his refusal. But Phocion was not to be **prevailed with** at all; and, shortly after, Alexander died.

Part Two

Phocion's house is seen yet at this day in the village of Melita, set forth with plates of copper, but otherwise plain and homely. For his wives, there is no mention made of the first, saving that Cephisodotus the image engraver was her brother. But for his second wife, she was no less famous at Athens for her honesty, and good housewifery, than Phocion for his justice and equity. And for proof thereof, it is reported, that the Athenians being one day assembled in the theater, to see new tragedies played, one of the players, when he should have come upon the **scaffold** to have played his part, asked Melanthius, the producer of the plays, for the apparel of a queen, and certain ladies to wait upon "her," because he was to play the part of the queen. Melanthius denying him this, the player went away in a rage, leaving the people staring one at another, and he would not come out upon the stage. But Melanthius, compelling him, brought him by force on the stage, and cried out unto him: "Dost thou not see Phocion's wife, that goeth up and down the city with one maid only waiting on her? and wilt thou play the fool, and mar the modesty of the women of Athens?" The people hearing his words, filled all the theater with joy and clapping of hands.

She herself, when a certain gentlewoman of Ionia came to Athens to see her, and showed her all her rich jewels and precious stones she had: she answered her again, "All my riches and jewels, is my husband Phocion, who these twenty years together, hath continually been chosen general for the Athenians."

Part Three

Phocion had a son named Phocus, who wished to take part in the games at **the great feast called the Panathenaea**. He permitted him so to do, in the contest of chariot-leaping, not with any view to the victory, but in the hope that the training and discipline for it would make him a better man, the youth being in a general way a lover of drinking, and **ill-regulated in his habits**. On his having succeeded in the sports, many were eager for the honour of his company at banquets, in celebration of the victory.

Phocion declined them all but one, and when he came to this entertainment and saw the costly preparations, even the water brought to wash the guests' feet being mingled with wine and spices, he reprimanded his son, asking him "How canst thou abide, Phocus, that our friend should thus disgrace thy victory with excess?" But because he would withdraw his son from such habits and company, he sent him to Sparta, and placed him there among young boys brought up **after the Laconian discipline**.

The Athenians were much offended at it, to see that Phocion did so much despise his own country's manner and fashions; and Demades twitted him with it publicly: "Suppose, Phocion, you and I advise the Athenians to adopt the Spartan constitution. If you like, I am ready to introduce a bill to that effect, and to speak in its favour." "Indeed," said Phocion, "you, with that strong scent of perfumes about you, and with that **mantle** on your shoulders, are just the very man to speak in honour of **Lycurgus**, and recommend the **Spartan table**."

Narration and Discussion

"He who needed not such gold and silver was richer than he that gave it to him." Explain.

"If I accept the gift," Phocion said, "I shall make all the city speak ill of the king and me both." Why might he have made this remark?

Describe Phocion's relationship with his son, perhaps using some form of **creative narration**. (Those who are curious might want to find out more about chariot-leaping.)

Lesson Seven

Introduction

In the year before Alexander died, his troublesome friend Harpalus finally went too far: he stole money from the king, ran away with it to Athens, and then used it to try to buy the Athenians' friendship. Those accused of accepting bribes from Harpalus included Demosthenes (who had to leave Athens for several months because he was unable to pay his fine), and Phocion's son-in-law Charicles; but Phocion himself remained uninterested in other people's money.

After the Harpalus scandal, the story moves quickly into the post-Alexander period, and the Lamian (or Hellenic) War, in which Athens and its allies fought Macedon and Boeotia for control of Greece.

Vocabulary

checked his proceedings: stopped what he was doing

constant: steady, unmovable

hustings: place from which speeches were made

think of it at better leisure…: Dryden, "There is no need to take counsel hastily or before it is safe."

insolently: arrogantly, rudely

for a furlong: The Athenians had sufficient resources for a short race, but not for a marathon.

when shall we leave to overcome?: "When can we stop having to have all these victories?"

People

Harpalus: an aristocrat of Macedon, and friend of Alexander

Leosthenes (#2): commander of the Greek forces in the Lamian War

Historic Occasions

324 B.C.: Harpalus' arrival in Athens

323 B.C.: Death of Harpalus (After being imprisoned in Athens and then escaping to Crete, he was murdered there.)

323 B.C.: Death of Alexander (as noted in the previous lesson)

323-322 B.C.: The Lamian War

323 B.C.: Death of Leosthenes

On the Map

province of Babylon: The kingdom of Babylon, which had ruled its own large empire but was now under Persian rule

Lamia: a city of central Greece

Reading

Part One

When Alexander wrote to demand a supply of galleys, and the orators objected to sending them, the people called upon Phocion chiefly to say his opinion. Phocion told them plainly, "Methinks ye must either make yourselves the strongest in wars, or, being the weaker, procure to be friends unto the stronger."

[omission for length and content]

And when **Harpalus**, King Alexander's lieutenant of the **province of Babylon**, fled out of Asia, and came to Attica with a great sum of gold and silver: straight away these men that sold their tongues to the people for money flocked about him like a flight of swallows. He gave every one of them a piece of money to bait them with: for it was a trifle to him, considering the great sums of money he brought. But to Phocion himself, he sent unto him seven hundred talents, and offered himself, and all that he had, into his hands of trust. But Phocion gave him a sharp answer, and told him that he would make him repent it if he corrupted the city of Athens in that manner. This, for the time, silenced Harpalus, and **checked his proceedings**.

But afterwards, when the Athenians were deliberating in council about him, he found those that had received money from him to be his greatest enemies, urging and aggravating matters against him to prevent themselves being discovered; whereas Phocion, who had never touched his pay, now, so far as the public interest would admit it, showed some regard to his particular security. This encouraged him once more to try his inclinations (to bribe Phocion); but he found him so **constant** that no money could carry the man.

Then Harpalus professed a particular friendship with Charicles (Phocion's son-in-law). And admitting him into his confidence in all his affairs, and continually requesting his assistance, he brought him under some suspicion *[omission for length and content]*. But when Charicles was called to account for his financial dealings with Harpalus, and entreated his father-in-law's protection, begging that he would appear for him in the court, Phocion refused, telling him, "I did not choose you for my son-in-law for any but honourable purposes."

Part Two

Asclepiades, the son of Hipparchus, brought the first news of the death of King Alexander; but Demades the orator would not believe him. "For," said he, "if it were true, all the earth would smell of the savour of his corpse." Phocion, seeing the people eager for an instant revolution, did his best to quiet and repress them; but numbers of them rushed up to the **hustings** to speak, and cried out that the news was true, and Alexander was dead. "Well then," quoth Phocion, "if it be true today, it shall be true also tomorrow, and the next day after. And therefore my masters, be not too hasty, but **think of it at better leisure, and set your affairs at a sure stay**."

Part Three

When **Leosthenes (#2)** now had embarked the city in the Lamian War, greatly against Phocion's wishes, he asked him scoffingly what the state had been benefited by his having now so many years been general. Phocion answered him, "No small good," said he, "for all my countrymen have been buried at home in their own graves." Another time, Leosthenes speaking proudly and **insolently** to the people, Phocion one day said unto him, "Young man, my friend, thy words are like to a cypress tree, which is high and great, but beareth no fruit." Then Hypereides rising up, asked Phocion, "When wilt thou then counsel the Athenians to make war?" "When I shall see young men," said he, "not forsake their ranks, rich men contribute their money, and the orators leave off robbing the treasury."

When the Athenians wondered to see such a goodly great army as Leosthenes had levied: and that they asked Phocion how he liked it: "A goodly army," quoth he, "**for a furlong**; but what I fear is the long race, for I do not see the city able to make any more money, nor more ships, neither yet any more soldiers than these." The which proved true, as it fell out afterwards. For at the first, Leosthenes did notable exploits. He overcame the Boeotians in battle, and drove Antipater into the city of **Lamia**: the which did put the Athenians in such a hope and jollity, that they made continual feasts and sacrifices through the city, to thank the gods for these good news. And there were some among them, that to convince Phocion of his error, asked him if he did not wish that he had done all those things? "Yes indeed," answered he, "I would I had done them; but yet I would not have given the counsel to have done them."

Another time also when letters came, daily, one after another, bringing "good news": "Good gods," said he, "**when shall we leave to overcome?**"

Leosthenes, soon after, was killed; and now those who feared that if Phocion obtained the command he would put an end to the war, arranged with an obscure person in the assembly, who should stand up and profess himself to be a friend and old schoolfellow of Phocion's, and persuade the people to spare him at this time, and reserve him (with whom none could compare) for a more pressing occasion; and now to give Antiphilus the command of the army. The people were contented withal. But then Phocion stood up, and said that this man was never scholar with him, neither did he ever know him before that time. "But now," said he, "from henceforth I will take thee for my friend, for thou hast given the people the best counsel for me."

Narration and Discussion

Why did Phocion not see the "good news" as something to rejoice at?

Some Athenians feared that Phocion would put an end to the war. Why might they want the war to continue?

Creative narration: Choose one of the stories told here about Phocion, and act it out, or retell it in some other way.

Creative narration for older students: Against each of the historical events described here, Plutarch has placed an anecdote about Phocion, or a quote from his reaction to those events. Try using a similar technique in something you are writing yourself (anything from a history essay to a piece of creative non-fiction, fiction, or poetry).

Lesson Eight

Introduction

Phocion, at the age of eighty, led the Athenians in a victory against Macedonian troops. The cities of Greece, however, were so disunified that, within a short time, they all fell under Macedonian rule. When the Athenians called on Phocion as the natural choice to lead peace talks with Antipater, he could not resist the chance to say "I told you so." However, he agreed, and the negotiations seemed to go well: perhaps too well. Some people worried that Phocion's friendship with the Macedonian commander might not be the best thing for Athens.

Vocabulary

threescore: sixty (so **fourscore** is eighty)

over-strait: too strict

pillage: robbery

who was no longer competent to vote in the assembly: Demades had temporarily lost his privileges in the government.

impunity: freedom from punishment or consequences

capitulations: terms, treaty

surrender at discretion: surrender unconditionally

Demosthenes and Hypereides should be delivered up to him: Phocion had managed to get the agitators out of similar trouble with Alexander; but this time their death warrants were non-negotiable.

that they should retain their ancient laws and government: Other sources say that the second term of the treaty was that only landowners would retain rights such as voting in the assembly.

receive a garrison into Munychia: Munychia was next to Piraeus, which functioned as the Athenian harbour. Antipater insisted on this representation as he expected to be occupied in Asia for some time.

People

Micion: a Macedonian general

Leonnatus, Craterus: former officers of Alexander

Historic Occasions

322 B.C.: Battle of Crannon

322 B.C.: Death of Leonnatus

On the Map

Rhamnus: or Rhamnous; a city overlooking the Euboean Strait

Reading

Part One

The people, notwithstanding, determining to make war with the Boeotians, Phocion spoke against it all he could. Thereupon, his friends bade him beware of such speeches: how he did offend the people, lest they kill him. He answered them, "They shall wrongfully put me to death, speaking for the benefit of my country; but otherwise they shall have reason to do it, if I speak to the contrary."

But when he saw nothing would pacify them, and that they went on still with their intent: then he commanded the herald to proclaim by sound of trumpet that all citizens from fourteen years to **threescore**, able to carry weapons, should presently, upon breaking up of the assembly, arm themselves, and follow him with five days' provision for victuals. Then was there great stir among them in the city, and the old men came and complained unto him for his over-**strait** commandment. He told them again, "I do you no wrong: for I am **fourscore** myself, and yet will go with you." This succeeded in pacifying them for the present.

But when **Micion**, with a large force of Macedonians and mercenaries, began to **pillage** the seacoast, having made a descent upon **Rhamnus**, and overrun the neighbouring country, Phocion led out the Athenians to attack him. But when he was there, some of his men taking upon them the office of a lieutenant, and going about to counsel him, some advising him to lodge his camp upon such a hill, and others to send his horsemen to such a place, and others to camp here: "O Hercules," quoth he, "how many captains do I see, and how few soldiers!"

Afterwards when he had set his footmen in battle array, there was one among them that left his rank, and stepped out before them all. Thereupon one of his enemies also made towards him, to fight with him: but the Athenian's heart failed him, and he went back again to his place. Then said Phocion unto him, "Art thou not ashamed, young lout, to have forsaken thy rank twice? the one where thy captain had placed thee, and the other in the which thou hadst placed thyself?"

However, he entirely routed the enemy, killing Micion and many more on the spot. The Grecian army also, in Thessaly, after **Leonnatus** and the Macedonians who came with him out of Asia had arrived and joined Antipater, fought and beat them in a battle. Leonnatus was killed in the fight, Antiphilus commanding the foot soldiers, and Menon the Thessalian, the horsemen.

Part Two

Shortly after, **Craterus** crossed out of Asia into Europe with a great army. A pitched battle was fought at **Crannon**; the Greeks were beaten; though not, indeed, in a signal defeat, nor with any great loss of men. But what with their want of obedience to their commanders, who were young and over-indulgent with them; and what with Antipater's tampering and treating with their separate cities: one by one, the end of it was that the army was dissolved, and the Greeks shamefully surrendered the liberty of their country.

Upon the news of Antipater's now advancing at once against Athens with all his force, Demosthenes and Hypereides deserted the city. Demades, who was in disgrace and defamed for lack of payment of such fines as were set upon his head (being seven different times condemned, because he had so many times moved matters contrary to the law) and **who was no longer competent to vote in the assembly**, laid hold of this season of **impunity** to bring in a bill for sending ambassadors unto Antipater, with full commission and authority to treat with him of peace. The people called for Phocion, calling him the person they only and entirely confided in. Then Phocion answered them: "If you had believed my former counsels I always gave you, such weighty matters should not now have troubled you at all." However, the vote passed; and a decree was made, and he with others were deputed to go to Antipater, who lay now encamped in the Theban territories, but intended to dislodge immediately, and pass into Attica.

Part Three

Phocion's first request to Antipater was that he would make the treaty without moving his camp. And when Craterus declared that it was not fair to ask them to be burdensome to the country of their friends and allies by their stay, when they might rather use that of their enemies for provisions and the support of their army, Antipater, taking him by the hand, said, "We must grant this favour to Phocion." And for the rest, touching the **capitulations** of peace, Antipater willed that the Athenians should return, and inform their people that he could only offer them the same terms (namely, to **surrender at discretion**) which Leosthenes had offered to him when he was besieged in the city of Lamia.

So when Phocion was come back to Athens, the Athenians, seeing there was no remedy, were compelled to be contented with such offers of peace as the enemy made them.

[Omission for length: the Athenians, including Phocion and Xenocrates the philosopher (see **Lesson One***), were sent on a second embassy to Antipater. Antipater sneered at Xenocrates, but was more willing to talk with Phocion.]*

When Phocion had declared the purpose of their embassy, Antipater replied shortly that he would make peace with the Athenians on these conditions, and no others: first, that **Demosthenes and Hypereides should be delivered up to him**; second, **that the Athenians should retain their ancient laws and government**; third, that they should **receive a garrison into Munychia**; and fourth, that they should pay a certain sum for the cost of the war. As things stood, these terms were judged tolerable by the rest of the ambassadors. Xenocrates the philosopher only said that "if Antipater considered the Athenians slaves, he was treating them fairly; but if free, severely." Phocion pressed Antipater only to spare them the garrison, and used many arguments and entreaties. Antipater replied, "Phocion, we are ready to do you any favour, saving that which should undo thee and us both."

[Omission for length: Plutarch explains that there are different versions of the meeting with Antipater, but that, in the end, the Athenians were forced to accept all the terms, including the garrison; and Menyllus, an honest man and friend of Phocion, was to be sent as its captain.]

Narration and Discussion

From an earlier lesson: "He knew also that Pallas, the goddess and protector of Athens, was ...skillful to rule both in war *and* peace." How did Phocion show that he was still a master of both?

Many Athenians blamed the ambassadors for giving in too easily; they felt they had been "sold out." Should they have tried harder to get a better outcome for their people?

Creative narration: You and a friend arrive in Athens before the official party returns, and people ask for the whole story. However, the two of you disagree on what was decided. Write or act out the scene.

Lesson Nine

Introduction

The Macedonian garrison arrived in Athens during a religious festival, which was considered not only in poor taste, but an unlucky omen as well. Life for many people became difficult: those forced to sell their land (because of the fines due to Antipater) also lost their right to hold public office and vote in the assembly, and many of them left the city. Those citizens who stayed and kept their privileges ruled Athens as an **oligarchy** (see introductory notes).

Phocion, stoic as always, took advantage of the opportunity to clean house, shuffling people he respected into government positions. Though he attempted to do what was best, he seemed oblivious to the anger brewing among those who had lost money and status.

Vocabulary

arbitrary: based on personal whim rather than reason

great festival: see **Lesson Two**

Iacchus: a minor deity worshipped as part of the Eleusinian Mysteries

profaned: defiled; treated as unholy

oppressed and shamefully used: Although these citizens managed to remain in the city, they had lost valued privileges such as voting in the assembly, holding public office, and serving on juries.

deaths of Demosthenes at Calauria, and of Hypereides at Cleonae: After receiving a death sentence, Demosthenes escaped to the island of Calauria; but when his hideout was discovered, he took poison and died. Hypereides was also put to death.

placable: forgiving, merciful

homely fare: simple diet

intercession: intervention, pleading on their behalf

preferring…to the magistracies: proposing men for public offices

busy and turbulent talkers: "Busy" can mean ready to serve, but also too much so ("pushy"); "turbulent talkers" are agitators.

strangers: foreigners, non-Athenians

deprecate: to criticize something; or to diminish, lessen its value

he could never satisfy him: Demades found life under Antipater quite enjoyable and financially rewarding; and he spent much of his time seeking out expensive pleasures, partly as revenge on those who had previously looked down on him.

People

Agnonides the sycophant: (or Hagnonides) An orator who was exiled to the Peloponnesus (but nowhere worse, thanks to Phocion's intervention). A **sycophant** can mean a flatterer, but in ancient Greece, **sycophants** like Agnonides were "false accusers," paid to initiate court cases by wealthy citizens who, for one reason or another, did not want to be publicly involved.

Xenocrates: a philosopher (see **Lesson One**)

Historic Occasions

322 B.C.: Deaths of Demosthenes and Hypereides

320 B.C.: Antipater made himself regent of Alexander's empire

On the Map

Thrace: see **Lesson Four**

mountains of Ceraunia: now part of Albania

Reading

Part One

This commandment to receive the garrison within Munychia seemed sufficiently imperious and **arbitrary**, indeed rather a spiteful and insulting way for Antipater to boast of his power, than for any profit could otherwise come of it. The resentment felt upon it was heightened by the time it happened in; for the garrison was brought in on the twentieth of the month of Boedromion, just at the time of the **great festival**, when they carry forth **Iacchus** with solemn pomp from the city to Eleusis; so that the solemnity being disturbed, many began to consider that, in old time when their realm did flourish, there were heard and seen voices and images of the gods on that day, which made the enemies both afraid, and amazed: and now in contrary manner, in the very selfsame solemnity of the gods, they saw the greatest calamity that could have happened unto Greece, the most holy time being **profaned**; and their greatest jubilee made the unlucky date of their most extreme calamity.

[omission for length and content]

Part Two

The garrison did not greatly offend nor trouble the Athenians, because of the honesty of their captain Menyllus. But those who had lost the benefit of their freedom by poverty amounted to more than twelve thousand; so that both those that remained in the city thought themselves **oppressed and shamefully used**; and those who on this account left their homes and went away into **Thrace**, where Antipater offered them a town and some territory to inhabit, regarded themselves only as a colony of slaves and exiles. And when to this was added the **deaths of Demosthenes at Calauria, and of Hypereides at Cleonae**, the citizens began to think with regret of Philip and Alexander, and almost to wish the return of those times *[omission for length]*. They remembered the contests they had with those kings, whose anger, however great, was yet generous and **placable**; whereas Antipater, with the counterfeit humility of appearing like a private man in the meanness of his dress and his **homely fare**, showed himself notwithstanding a more cruel lord and tyrant unto them whom he had overcome.

Yet Phocion had influence with him to recall many from banishment by his **intercession**, and those whom he could not get to be restored, yet he procured that they should not be banished into such far countries as others which had been sent beyond Taenarus, and the **mountains of Ceraunia**; but that they could remain in Greece, and plant themselves within the country of Peloponnesus: among the which was **Agnonides the sycophant**.

He was no less studious to manage the affairs within the city with equity and moderation, **preferring** constantly those that were men of worth and good education **to the magistracies**, and recommending that the **busy and turbulent talkers**, to whom it was a mortal blow to be excluded from office and public debating, should learn to stay at home, and be content to till their land.

When he saw **Xenocrates** also pay a certain tax to the commonwealth, which all **strangers** dwelling in Athens did use yearly to pay: he would have made him a free man, and offered to put his name amongst the number of free citizens. But Xenocrates refused it, saying he would have no part of that freedom which he had been sent as an ambassador to **deprecate**. And when Menyllus wished to give Phocion money, he replied that Menyllus was no greater lord than Alexander had been, neither had he at that time any greater occasion to receive his present than when he had refused King Alexander's gift. Menyllus replying again, said that if he had no need of it for himself, yet he might let his son Phocus have it. But Phocion answered: "If my son returns to a right mind, that which I will leave him shall serve his turn very well: but if it be so that he will still hold on the course he hath taken, there is no riches then that can suffice him."

But to Antipater he answered more sharply, who would have him engaged in something dishonourable. "Antipater," said he, "cannot have me both as his friend and his flatterer." And, indeed, Antipater was wont to say he had two friends at Athens, Phocion and Demades; of the which, he could never make the one to take anything of him, and the other, **he could never satisfy him**.

And truly Phocion's poverty was a great glory of his virtue, since he was grown old, continuing in the same, after he had been so many times general of the Athenians, and had received such friendship and courtesy, of so many kings and princes.

[omission for length]

Narration and Discussion

The Athenians remembered Philip and Alexander as "generous and placable," at least in comparison to Antipater. Would you agree?

Antipater said that he considered Phocion a friend, although he was frustrated by his inability to be bribed. Did this put Phocion in a safe place, or a dangerous one?

For older students: Considering Phocion's philosophy on politics and other matters, is it unsurprising that he was a bit callous about those who had lost their right to participate in government?

Creative narration #1: You are an Athenian a) political cartoonist, or b) musician. Express your views about the current situation.

Lesson Ten

Introduction

Another change in power took place with the death of Antipater. Things got a bit confusing, as Demades, expecting an interview with Antipater, met his death at his son Cassander's hands instead.

The conflict over Antipater's successor divided even the Athenians. The wealthier "oligarchic" party (including Phocion) supported Cassander, who had never risen above second place in anything, but who nevertheless expected to take over his father's position as "Keeper of the Kings." Antipater, however, had named his general Polyperchon to succeed him. In an attempt to win over the disadvantaged citizens, and rid himself of troublemakers like Phocion, Polyperchon promised to end the unpopular oligarchy, bring home the exiles, and restore democracy in Athens: but only as long as they promised never to rebel against Macedon.

One point to remember is that Athens, though it considered itself all-important, was only one element in the huge competition for the pieces of Alexander's empire. In the "Macedonian News," struggles in Greece probably earned minor headlines in comparison with bigger battles. However, as this is a *Life* and not a volume of world history, we will continue to focus on Athens, and particularly on Phocion.

Vocabulary

great grievance: It was particularly worrisome because the Macedonians, controlling the harbour, could cut off food supplies.

office: task

when Antipater was already seized with a sickness: Antipater was still alive, but Cassander was managing his affairs.

entrusted…: see "The Kings of Macedon," below

countermine Cassander: To **countermine** is to defeat someone by making secret plans against them. Cassander, unwilling to act as second-in-command to Polyperchon, was busy making alliances and raising military support of his own.

wile and crafty fetch: scheme, trick

fill the city with a crowd…: bring in many people who had some grievance against the government, and Phocion in particular

affront: insult

transgressing: breaking

hoped by professions of confidence…: Phocion hoped that by demonstrating trustworthiness, he would receive the same in return.

credulity and confidence in him: Plutarch says that it was a fatal mistake to trust in Nicanor's good intentions toward Athens.

overweening: overly confident

sundry intimations: various hints

attack Piraeus: If Nicanor could gain control of the harbour, he would be able to keep Polyperchon's ships out, and at the same time he would be able to threaten rebellious Athenians with a food blockade.

be ready to follow Phocion their general: that is, Phocion was ordered to lead an attack on Nicanor

drew trenches about Piraeus: seized the harbour

pretending to aid them…: Alexander took control of Athens.

disfranchised persons: deprived of the rights belonging to citizens

a motley and irregular public assembly: a disorderly group; a mob

divested Phocion: It seems that Phocion was not only stripped of his position and property, but forced to flee the city.

alone in close conference with Nicanor: Phocion was in charge of arranging public peace negotiations between Nicanor and Alexander; but when the two were found to be already conferring privately, the Athenians blamed Phocion for deceiving them.

Note on the Diadochi

The Greek word *Diadochi* (pronounced dye-AD-a-kee) means "successors." It refers to the family and friendsof Alexander who battled for control of his empire: the list included Antipater, Craterus, Perdiccas, Leonnatus, Antigonus, Polyperchon, and Cassander. The Wars of the Diadochi lasted from 322 until 281 B.C.

Note on the Kings of Macedon

King Philip II of Macedon was succeeded by his son Alexander III (The Great). But what happened after that?

Alexander died without a clear heir to his throne, although his wife was expecting a child. His older half-brother Arrhidaeus became king (he was officially called Philip III), but due to a disability he was unable to rule completely, and most of the decisions were made by regents (Perdiccas, Antipater, and finally Polyperchon).

The son born after Alexander's death also had people who supported his right to the throne over that of his uncle; and after Philip III was put to death in 317 B.C., he became King Alexander IV, and "ruled" until he was murdered in 310 or 309 B.C.

And what about Cassander? He essentially ruled Macedon from 317 B.C. until he was formally made king in 305. (He died in 297 B.C.)

People

Cassander: son of Antipater and later king of Macedon (see above). As a boy, he had been a student of **Aristotle** along with **Alexander**.

Antigonus: Antigonus I Monopthalmus, a former general of Alexander.

Polyperchon: sometimes spelled Polysperchon; a Macedonian general

Nicanor: There were various people by this name, but this Nicanor is the one known as an Antipatrid General (i.e. supporting Antipater and then Cassander). He was put to death by Cassander in 317 B.C.

Historic Occasions

319 B.C.: Death of Antipater

319 or 318 B.C.: Murder of Demades by Cassander

318 B.C.: Polyperchon restored Athenian liberties

On the Map

Pella: the Macedonian capital

Salamis: a large island in the Aegean Sea

Reading

Part One

The garrison in Munychia continued to be felt as a **great grievance**, and the Athenians were importunate with Phocion to go to Antipater, to entreat him to take his garrison out of their city. Phocion declined the **office**, either because he had no hope to obtain it, or for that he saw the people more obedient unto reason for fear of the garrison. Howbeit he contented himself with obtaining of Antipater the postponement, for the present, of the payment of the sum of money in which the city was fined.

So the Athenians perceiving they could do no good with Phocion, they entreated Demades, who willingly took the matter upon him, and went with his son into Macedon; and some superior power, as it seems, so ordering it, he came to **Pella** just at the time **when Antipater was already seized with a sickness** whereof he died. The affairs of the realm, therefore, went through the hands of **Cassander** his son, who had found a letter from Demades, formerly written by him to **Antigonus** in Asia, willing him to come in all possible speed to win Greece and Macedon, which hung but of an old rotten thread, mocking Antipater in this manner.

[Omission for content: the deaths of Demades and his son at the hands of Cassander.]

Part Two

Now Antipater, before his death, had established **Polyperchon** as general of the army of the Macedonians, and Cassander, his son, only as colonel of a thousand footmen. He, notwithstanding, after his father's decease taking upon him the government of the realm, sent **Nicanor** with speed to succeed Menyllus in the captainship of the garrison of Athens, before Antipater's death should be revealed; commanding him first, in any case, to take the fort of Munychia, which he did. Shortly after, the Athenians understanding of the death of Antipater, they accused Phocion, for that he had known of his death long before, and yet kept it secret to please Nicanor. But he slighted their talk, and making it his duty to visit and confer continually with Nicanor, he succeeded in procuring his goodwill and kindness for the Athenians, and induced him even to put himself to trouble and expense to seek popularity with them, by presiding at the games.

In the meantime Polyperchon, who was **entrusted with the charge of the king**, to **countermine Cassander**, sent a letter to the city, declaring, in the name of the king, that he restored them their democracy, and that the whole Athenian people were at liberty to conduct their commonwealth according to their ancient customs and constitutions. But this was a **wile and crafty fetch** against Phocion. For Polyperchon, devising this practice to get the city of Athens into his hands (as it fell out afterwards by proof), had no hope to obtain his purpose, unless he found means first to banish Phocion; and the most certain way to ruin him would be again to **fill the city with a crowd of disfranchised citizens, and let loose the tongues of the demagogues and common accusers**.

With this prospect the Athenians were all in excitement, and Nicanor, wishing to confer with them on the subject, at a meeting of the council in Piraeus, came himself, trusting for the safety of his person to Phocion. And when Dercyllus, who commanded the guard there, made an attempt to seize him, upon notice of it beforehand, he made his escape; and there was little doubt he would now lose no time in righting himself upon the city for the **affront**; and when Phocion was found fault with for letting him get away and not securing him, he defended himself by saying that he had no mistrust of Nicanor, nor the least reason to expect any mischief from him, but should it prove otherwise, for his part he would have them all know he would rather receive than do the wrong.

And so far as he spoke for himself alone, the answer was honourable and high-minded enough; but he who hazards his country's safety, and that, too, when he is her magistrate and chief commander, can scarcely be acquitted, I fear, of **transgressing** a higher and more sacred obligation of justice, which he owed to his fellow-citizens. For it will not even do to say that he dreaded involving the city in war, by seizing Nicanor, and **hoped by professions of confidence and just-dealing to retain him in the observance of the like**; but it was, indeed, his **credulity and confidence in him**, and an **overweening** opinion of his sincerity, that imposed upon him.

Part Three

Thus, notwithstanding the **sundry intimations** Phocion had of Nicanor's preparations to **attack Piraeus**, sending soldiers over into **Salamis**, and tampering with and endeavouring to corrupt various residents in Piraeus, he would, notwithstanding all this evidence, never be persuaded to believe it. And even when Philomedes of Lampra had got a decree passed that all the Athenians should stand to their arms, and **be ready to follow Phocion their general**, he yet sat still and did nothing, until Nicanor actually led his troops out from Munychia, and **drew trenches about Piraeus**. But then, when Phocion thought to lead out the people to prevent him, he found they mutinied against him, and no man would obey his commandment.

[Plutarch neglects to mention that Nicanor received a royal order to surrender the harbour and dissolve the garrison. Nicanor said he would obey the order, but seemed to be stalling on doing anything about it. It seemed likely that he was waiting for Polyperchon to send troops to keep the peace as democracy was restored.]

In the meantime, Alexander the son of Polyperchon came with an army, **pretending to aid them of the city against Nicanor**; where indeed he meant (if he could) to get the rest of the city into his hands, whilst they were in tumult and divided among themselves. For all those that had previously been expelled from the city now coming back with him, made their way into it, and they were joined by a mixed multitude of foreigners and **disfranchised persons**, and of these **a motley and irregular public assembly** came together, in which they **divested Phocion of all power**, and chose other generals. And if by chance Alexander had not been spied from the walls, **alone in close conference with Nicanor**; and had not this, which was often repeated, given the Athenians cause of suspicion; the city would not have escaped the snare.

Narration and Discussion

The political and military maneuvers described here may seem too complicated to follow easily, and many Athenians must have thought so as well. Which Macedonian rulers had their best interests at heart? What local leaders were to be trusted? Would they ever be independent again? Phocion, as "magistrate and chief commander" of Athens, had an additional "high and sacred obligation" to pursue justice for his people, rather than worrying about his own safety. How would you rate his actions during this time? Did he deserve to lose his position?

Why might the oligarchs have felt extremely concerned about the return to public life of the "disfranchised persons?"

For further thought: Christian students might want to examine what the Bible says about trusting in good intentions vs. gullibility (1 Corinthians 13:7, Matthew 10:16).

Lesson Eleven

Introduction

Phocion, suddenly jobless and homeless, decided to plead his case, or at least beg for shelter, at the court of the Macedonian king.

Vocabulary

impeached him of treason: accused him of treason for his initial refusal and then his delay to attack Nicanor

consulted their own security: tried to save themselves

went over to Polyperchon: Phocion, rejected by the Athenians, decided to seek refuge with Polyperchon at **Phocis.**

put to death: Other sources say that Dinarchus, if it was the same person, died much later in Athens.

shut up together in one cage: North's translation says "Put us all in prison, and then send us bound hands and feet to Athens."

Phocion struck his staff on the ground...: Others say that it was Polyperchon who struck his scepter on the ground.

seized: arrested

bondmen: slaves or indentured servants

People

Agnonides: see **Lesson Nine**. Agnonides had just returned from exile, but he had already gained a high position in the assembly.

Callimedon: Callimedon, nicknamed "the Crab" or "Spiny Lobster" because of his fondness for eating seafood, was a member of the pro-Macedonian party (he had been charged previously with conspiracy against the Athenian government).

Charicles: probably Phocion's son-in-law Charicles

Dinarchus: or Deinarchus; a speech-writer for other orators (since he was not Athenian, he was not allowed to participate in the debates)

Archestratus: a member of the ruling council in Athens.

Hegemon: one of Phocion's group

Cleitus ("the White"): a Macedonian general who was responsible for bringing the prisoners back to Athens and reading the charges against them; however, their ultimate fate was left to the "democracy" of the Athenians.

Historic Occasions

317 B.C.-c. 311 B.C.: Polyperchon's fleet was destroyed by Antigonus; Cassander took control of Athens; Polyperchon fled first to Epirus, then to the Peloponnesus where he allied himself with Antigonus and took control of that region.

On the Map

Phocis (Phocians): a region of central Greece

Pharygae: The exact location is uncertain.

Reading

Part One

The orator **Agnonides** at once fell foul upon Phocion, and **impeached him of treason**. **Callimedon** and **Charicles**, fearing the worst, **consulted their own security** by fleeing from the city. Phocion, with a few of his friends that stayed with him, **went over to Polyperchon**; and, out of respect for him, Solon of Plataea and **Dinarchus** of Corinth, who were reputed friends and confidants of Polyperchon, accompanied him. But because Dinarchus fell sick by the way, in the city of Elatea, they stayed there many days, hoping of his recovery.

But in the meantime, the people, at the persuasion of the orator Agnonides and at the request of **Archestratus**, established a decree to send delegates unto Polyperchon, to accuse Phocion. So both parties reached Polyperchon at the same time, who was going through the country with the king, and was then at a small village of **Phocis**, called **Pharygae**, under the mountain now called Galate, but then called Acrurium. There Polyperchon commanded a golden canopy to be set up, and caused the king to be set under the same, and all his chiefest friends about him. He ordered Dinarchus at once to be taken, tortured, and **put to death**; and that done, he gave audience to the Athenians, who filled the place with noise and tumult, accusing and recriminating on one another; till at last Agnonides came forward, and requested they might all be **shut up together in one cage**, and conveyed to Athens, there to decide the controversy. The king laughed to hear him say so.

But the noblemen of Macedon that were present then, and divers strangers besides to hear their complaints, made sign to the ambassadors to go on with their case at once. But it was no sort of fair hearing. Polyperchon frequently interrupted Phocion, till at last **Phocion struck his staff on the ground, and declined to speak further**. And when **Hegemon** also told Polyperchon that he himself could best witness how Phocion had always faithfully served and loved the people: he angrily answered him, "Come not hither to lie falsely to me, in the presence of the king." Therewith the king rose out of his seat, and took a spear in his hand, thinking to have killed Hegemon, had not Polyperchon suddenly interposed and hindered him; so that the assembly dissolved.

Phocion, then, and those about him, were **seized**; those of his friends that were not immediately by him, on seeing this, hid their faces, and saved themselves by flight. Those remaining were brought to Athens, to be submitted to trial; but, in truth, as men already sentenced to die.

[omission for length]

Part Two

The king's letters were read openly to the Athenians, by the which he did advertise the people that he had found these offenders convicted of treason: notwithstanding, that he referred the sentence of their condemnation unto them, for that they were free men. Then **Cleitus** brought the prisoners before the people.

Every respectable citizen, at the sight of Phocion, covered up his face, and stooped down to conceal his tears. One of them had the courage to say, "My lords, since the king referreth the judgement of so great persons unto the people, it were great reason all the **bondmen** and strangers, which are no free citizens of Athens, should be taken out of this assembly." The people would not agree to it, but cried out that such traitors should be stoned to death that favour the authority of a few, and are enemies of the people; whereupon silence was made, and no man dared speak any more in support of Phocion.

Phocion was with difficulty heard at all, when he asked them: "My lords, will ye put us to death lawfully or unlawfully?" Some answered him: "According to law." "How then can ye do it," quoth he, "that will not hear our justifications?" But when they were deaf to all he said, approaching nearer, "As to myself," said he, "I admit my guilt, and have in government committed faults deserving death: but for these prisoners with me, what have they done, why you should put them to death?" The common people answered him, "Because they are thy friends." With this answer Phocion drew back, and spoke never a word more.

Then Agnonides, holding a decree in his hand, read it openly to the people, declaring how they should be judged by show of hands, whether the offenders had deserved death or not: and if it were found they had, then that they should all be put to death. When this had been read out, some desired it might be added to the sentence, that before Phocion should be put to death, they should first torture him *[omission for content]*. But Agnonides perceiving that even Cleitus was offended with it, and thinking besides it were too beastly and barbarous a part to use him in that sort, he said openly: "My lords, when you shall have such a varlet in your hands as Callimedon, then you may cast him on the wheel: but against Phocion, I would not act with such cruelty." Then rose up a nobleman among them, and added to his words: "Thou hast reason to say so, Agnonides: for if Phocion should be laid on the wheel, what should we then do with thee?"

[Omission for length: the decree was passed, and all the men were condemned to death.]

Narration and Discussion

Plutarch framed this story in ways that elicit sympathy for Phocion: for example, in an omitted passage, he describes how the prisoners were bumped through the marketplace in wagons, past a jeering crowd; however, he neglects to point out that a "wagon" may have been necessary due to Phocion's advanced age. Can you find other examples that may also have reasonable explanations?

Was the anger of the Athenians justified? Should Phocion's actions in his final years have been balanced against his lifetime of effort on behalf of Athens? Older students may examine these questions in essay format or as a debate.

Lesson Twelve and Examination Questions

Introduction

This final lesson describes the death of Phocion (which was not without its moments of humour), and its aftermath.

Vocabulary

magnanimity: "spirit of greatness," in this context meaning nobility, the ability to rise above the situation

reviling and abusing: insulting, mocking

hemlock: a highly poisonous plant

mortar: a bowl used for crushing herbs or preparing medicine

drachma: a unit of money

debauched: corrupted; made immoral

impiously: against religious beliefs

hearth: a fireplace in the home

relics: remains

People

a gentlewoman of Megara: Dryden says that it was Phocion's wife

Epicurus and **Demophilus:** two others who had prosecuted Phocion

Socrates: a famous philosopher who was executed by the same method

Historic Occasions

318 B.C.: Death of Phocion

Reading

After the assembly was dismissed, they were carried to the prison; the rest with cries and lamentations, their friends and relatives following and clinging about them; but Phocion, looking (as men observed with astonishment at his calmness and **magnanimity**), just the same as when he had been used to return to his home attended, as general, from the assembly. His enemies ran along by his side, **reviling and abusing** him; amongst whom there was one that stepped before him, and did spit in his face, at which Phocion, turning to the officers, only said, "You should stop this indecency."

When they were in prison, Thudippus seeing the **hemlock** which they brewed in a **mortar** to give them to drink, gave way to his passion, and began to bemoan his condition and the hard measure he received, saying that they wrongfully put him to death with Phocion. "You cannot be contented," said he (Phocion), "to die with Phocion?"

When one that stood by asked Phocion if he would say anything to his son Phocus: "Yes," quoth he, "that I will: bid him never revenge the wrong the Athenians do me."

Then Nicocles, one of Phocion's dearest friends, prayed him to let him drink the poison before him. Phocion answered him, "Thy request is grievous to me, Nicocles; but because I never denied thee anything in my life, I will also grant thee this at my death."

When all the rest had drunk, there was no more poison left, and the executioner said he would make no more unless they gave him twelve **drachmas** to defray the cost of the quantity required. Some delay was made, and time spent, until Phocion called one of his friends, and, observing that a man could not even die at Athens without paying for it, requested him to give the sum.

It was the nineteenth day of the month of Munychion (to wit, March), on which day it was the custom to have a solemn procession in the city, in honour of Jupiter. The horsemen, as they passed by, some of them threw away their garlands. Others stopped, weeping, and casting sorrowful looks towards the prison doors; and all the citizens whose minds were not absolutely **debauched** by spite and passion, or who had any humanity left, acknowledged it to have been most **impiously** done, not, at least, to let that day pass, and the city so be kept pure from death and a public execution at the solemn festival.

His enemies notwithstanding, continuing still their anger against him, made the people pass a decree that his body should be banished, and carried out of the bounds of the country of Attica, forbidding the Athenians that no fire should be made for the solemnizing of his funerals. For this respect no friend of his dared touch his body. Howbeit a poor man called Conopion, that was wont to get his living that way, being hired for money to burn men's bodies: he carried the body beyond Eleusis, and getting fire out of a woman's house of Megara, he solemnized his funerals.

Furthermore, there was **a gentlewoman of Megara**, who coming by chance that way, with her gentlewomen, where his body was but newly burnt: she caused the earth to be cast up a little where the body was burnt, and made it like to a hollow tomb, whereupon she did use such sprinklings and effusions as are commonly done at the funerals of the dead: and then taking up his bones in her lap in the night, she brought them home, and buried them in her **hearth**, saying: "O dear hearth, to thee I bequeath the **relics** of this noble and good man, and pray thee to keep them faithfully, to bring them one day to the grave of his ancestors, when the Athenians shall come to confess the fault and wrong they have done unto him."

And, indeed, a very little time and their own sad experience soon informed them that they had put him to death who only maintained justice and honesty at Athens. Whereupon they made his image to be set up in brass, and gave honourable burial to his bones, at the charges of the city. And for his accusers, they condemned Agnonides of treason, and put him to death themselves. The other two, **Epicurus** and **Demophilus**, being fled out of the city, were afterwards met with by his son Phocus, who was revenged of them.

[omission for length and content]

Furthermore, this death of Phocion did also revive the memory of the lamentable death of **Socrates** unto the Grecians, the two cases being so similar; and both equally the sad fault and misfortune of Athens.

Narration and Discussion

How did Phocion apply his Stoic beliefs even at this time?

At the time of Phocion's execution, the Athenians were quite certain that they were in the right. What made them later change their minds?

For older students: Plutarch began this *Life* by saying that it is better to struggle against disaster (even if you lose) than to *be* a walking disaster (like Demades). He suggested that Phocion, under different circumstances, might have been more successful, and that his gifts might have been more recognized. Do you agree?

Examination Questions

Younger Students:

1. The orator Demosthenes was known to say about Phocion, "See, the axe of my words riseth." What did he mean?

2. Tell about the friendship between Phocion and Alexander the Great.

Older Students:

1. How did Phocion apply his Stoic beliefs even when being put to death?; OR answer Question 2.

2. (High school) Phocion borrowed a life motto from the goddess Athena: "Skillful to rule in war and peace." Was he successful?

Marcus Furius Camillus

(c. 446/445-365 B.C.)

Who was Camillus?

Marcus Furius Camillus was a statesman and general of the early Roman Republic, referred to during his own lifetime as the "Second Founder of Rome." Camillus repeatedly held the high-ranking positions of **dictator** and **consular tribune** (see below), but (as Plutarch explains in the first lesson), the times he lived in prevented him from becoming a **consul**.

For those who have read Plutarch's *Life of Coriolanus*, Camillus was born about half a century after the Siege of Corioli. His family, the Furii, were of the **patrician** class, and his father was also one of the **consular tribunes**.

Who were the patricians and the plebeians?

There were two different types of class divisions in ancient Rome. The first was family-based, between the **patricians** (the nobility) and the **plebeians** (common people). The second type of division was between property- or wealth-based classes (such as the *senatores*), but it is less important than the first one in this story.

Why was Camillus a dictator, and why was that all right?

This story takes place during a time when certain Roman **consuls** had been suspected of conspiring to bring back the monarchy, and when there were frequent wars with other tribes. The office of *praetor maximus*, or **dictator**, was created as a safeguard: someone who would act as the supreme magistrate of the city, and also as its military general, for a limited period of time. The dictator was also referred to as *magister populi*, or "master of the infantry," and therefore his second-in-command was "master of the horse."

Most Roman dictatorships took place during the first two hundred years of the Republic; the position became much less common in later times (Fabius, Sulla, and Julius Caesar were among the later dictators).

What were the magistracies in Rome?

The elected positions, or magistracies, in the Roman Republic were (starting at the bottom) quaestor, aedile, praetor, and consul. (The office of tribune was a separate position, explained below.) There were various numbers of each of these: for example, two **consuls** were elected each year, and (at least at the beginning) they acted as judges and military generals as well as city leaders. (The historian Livy wrote that the office of **praetor**, intended to relieve the consuls of their judicial duties, was created near the end of Camillus' lifetime.)

In addition to overseeing the **census** (counting the citizens), the **censor** was responsible for public morality, which is where we get the word **censorship**. The office of censor was usually held by men of the **patrician** class who had previously been consuls; but there were exceptions such as Camillus, who was censor in 403 B.C. before becoming **consular tribune** in 401.

Who were the tribunes?

The civil office of **tribune of the plebeians**, or **tribune of the people**, was a "watchdog" position defending the rights of the common people, which had been established some years previously (see Plutarch's *Life of Coriolanus*). However, a **military tribune** was an army officer (ranking below a legate and above a centurion).

And to add to the confusion, this *Life* gives us a third version. A bill brought to the Senate at about the time Camillus was born proposed, first of all, intermarriage between the patrician and plebeian classes; and, second, that one of the two consuls could or should be from the plebeian class. The senators (all patricians) were not willing to accept this proposal, but they did offer a compromise: **consular tribunes** ("military tribunes with consular powers") would be elected in place of the consuls; and they could be of either class. This alternative election took place about half the time over the next few decades. The problem was that most of those elected either as consuls or tribunes were still patricians. Nothing had really changed. As Plutarch explains in **Lesson One**, Camillus could have run for consul when the position was open, but he chose not to because of the controversy surrounding it.

In 376 B.C., when Camillus was seventy years old, the **tribunes of the people** brought forward a proposal saying that one of the two consuls *must* (not just *could*) be from the plebeian class (see **Lesson Twelve**). When the Senate refused this demand, the people rebelled and managed to prevent regular elections from taking place for the next several years. Finally, with the support of Camillus (who had been appointed **dictator** again), the law was changed, plebeian consuls began to be elected, and the need for **consular tribunes** ended.

Nations Around Rome

As the story of Camillus belongs to an earlier time than many of Plutarch's other *Lives*, we hear about less-familiar rival tribes who eventually became part of the Roman Republic.

Aequi or **Aequians:** An **Italic** tribe who lived to the east of Rome

Italic: Like **Latin**, this refers to the Indo-European people who spoke **Italic** languages (there were other **Italic** languages besides Latin).

Etrurian, **Etruscan:** an ancient civilization in Italy, predating Rome

Gauls: Celtic tribes from the north, known for their strength in battle.

Latin: The name Latin (sometimes **Latian**) refers to an ancient Indo-European people who moved into the Italian peninsula during the late Bronze Age (1200-900 B.C.), and lived in a region they called Latium. From about 600 B.C. on, the Romans became the most powerful of the Latin tribes.

Volsci, Volscians: The Volsci were an **Italic** people who lived to the southwest of Rome. (North calls them the **Volsces.**)

A Special Note on Historical Problems

Those recording early history, and later interpreters and synthesizers such as Plutarch, sometimes repeated events, or put the same event in different places at different times. In this story, starting in **Lesson Nine**, Plutarch describes sieges and battles occurring at **Sutrium**. However, other sources record similar events at **Satricum**, leading later historians to wonder if Plutarch's cutting and pasting from various sources confused names and events.

I would suggest not trying to examine these military events too closely, for the reasons already explained. For simplicity, we will use the name **Sutrium**, and assume that events happened in the order related by Plutarch.

Top Vocabulary Terms in the Life of Camillus

If you know these words, you're well on the way to mastering the vocabulary for this study. They will not be repeated in the lessons.

1. **confederates:** allies, friends

2. **divination:** foretelling the future by interpreting omens

3. **hard by:** near to

4. **indigent:** poor, needy

5. **lusty:** strong, bold. To do something **lustily** is to do so energetically, with great force. The English word originally meant healthy, vigorous, even merry (which is why we might read that someone was singing **lustily**). The more negative meaning of **lust** (desire) seems to have come into use later on.

6. **practice, practise:** plan, plot, scheme. British/Canadian spelling differentiates between the noun and the verb; Americans use **practice** for both. It is also used in the more common way: in **Lesson Three**, the traitorous schoolmaster accustoms his pupils "by practice" to play near enemy lines.

7. **rash:** thoughtless; without the considering the consequences of an action

8. **siege:** the process of surrounding a city, or a fortified place such as a castle, to force it to surrender. The verb form is to **besiege** or to **lay siege to** it.

9. **spoil(s):** treasure or loot taken during a raid or after a battle.

10. **suffer:** allow, permit

P.S. on pesky apostrophes

"Camillus" is one of those names that cause debate about the proper way to show it in the possessive. Different style guides have different rules. For consistency, I have used the "apostrophe only" rule, but you may prefer to add an extra "s."

Lesson One

Introduction

This lesson may seem, at first reading, to be a disjointed start to the story of Camillus. We first read Plutarch's prologue about the many offices and commissions that he was given during his lifetime; then we hear just a bit about the military career that took up most of the first half of his life. By the end of Lesson One, we see Camillus leading the Roman army in a siege against troublesome rival cities; but Plutarch then veers off into the decision to build a drainage tunnel from the flooded Lake Albano, in hopes that certain prophecies of victory would then come true. The water story seems to end there, as Plutarch then moves on to the rest of the war (in **Lesson Two**).

With the lack of attention on Camillus himself, **Lesson One** may best be used as an introduction to life in Rome (and its neighbouring city-states) around 400 B.C. What can we tell already about Roman political issues, economic activities, religious beliefs, and methods of warfare? Which of these seem to be the most important? Which might cause conflict with others? And why might the Romans decide that they needed a dictator? See also the activities listed under **On the Map**.

Vocabulary

dictator, consul, *Tribuni militares*, censor: see introductory notes

had triumphed: had been given a parade honouring a military victory

the people: the plebeian class (see introductory notes)

at dissension: in conflict

odious: unpleasant, detestable

oligarchy: government by a small number of people

the government in the meantime…: during this time, there were some periods when they did elect consuls

against the inclination of the people: It was not that the common people did not want Camillus to be consul, but that they were protesting against the whole system.

honest: honourable

rated: put on the list of taxpayers

exempted from taxes: did not have to pay them

corn: grain, such as wheat or barley

portend: foretell, predict

prodigy: unusual occurrence

the oracle of Apollo, at the city of Delphi: a Greek temple famous for prophetic messages

Historic Occasions

509 B.C.: Founding of the Roman Republic

c. 446/445 B.C.: Birth of Camillus

445 B.C.: Decision to create consular tribunes (see introductory notes)

406 B.C.: Rome declared war against Veii

403 B.C.: Camillus was censor

401 B.C., 398 B.C.: Camillus was consular tribune (and head of the Roman army)

395/393 B.C.: Irrigation tunnel built from Lake Albano

On the Map

As an introduction to this study, it would be good not only to look at maps of the early Roman Republic and its surroundings (including bodies of water such as the Mediterranean, Adriatic, and Tuscan seas), but to review or become familiar with the city of Rome itself. If you are learning in a group, individual students or partners might be asked to research and briefly describe sites such as the Forum and the Capitoline Hill. (Remember that some famous features of Rome were not built until much later.)

Veii (Veians): an Etrurian city northwest of Rome

Tuscany: a region of central Italy

Falerii (Falerians): an Etrurian city northeast of Rome, and an ally of Veii, within the territory of the **Faliscans**

Capena (Capenates): a town just north of Rome, another ally of Veii

Alban lake: Lake Albano, a volcanic crater lake southeast of Rome

Reading

Prologue

[If this section causes confusion, please read the explanation in the general notes.]

Amongst many great matters which are spoken of Furius Camillus, this seemeth most strange and wonderful above the rest. That he, having borne the chiefest offices of charge in his country, and having done many notable and worthy deeds in the same; as one that was chosen five times **dictator**, and had **triumphed** four times, and had won himself the name and title of the "Second Founder of Rome"; and yet never came to be **consul**. But the only cause thereof was, that the commonwealth of Rome stood then in such state and sort that **the people** were then **at dissension** with the Senate, and would choose no more consuls, but another kind of magistrates whom they called ***Tribuni militares*** or military tribunes. These did all things with like power and authority as the consuls, yet were they not so **odious** unto the people, because it was divided among a large number. For it was some hope to the opponents of **oligarchy** that the government of the state being put into six, and not into two officers' hands, their rule would be the easier, and more tolerable. This was the condition of the times when Camillus was in the height of his actions and glory; and, although **the government in the meantime had often proceeded to consular elections**, yet he could never persuade himself to be consul **against the inclination of the people** *[omission for length]*.

Part One

[Omission for length: Plutarch says that Camillus distinguished himself in military service, and that he was honoured by being made ***censor*** *(in his forties).]*

In his office of censorship, Camillus did two notable acts. The one was very **honest**: he brought men that were not married to marry the women whom the wars had left widows, which were in number many. To this he got them partly by persuasion, and partly by threatenings, to set round fines upon their heads that refused. The other was very necessary, in causing orphans to be **rated**, who before were **exempted**

from taxes, the frequent wars requiring more than ordinary expenses to maintain them.

What, however, pressed them most was the siege of **Veii**. This was the head city of **Tuscany**, not inferior to Rome either in number of arms or multitude of soldiers. For the Veians were grown to stomach and courage in time, by reason of their wealth and prosperity, and for the sundry great battles they had fought against the Romans, that contended with them for glory and empire. It now it fell so out that, finding themselves weakened by many great overthrows which they had received of the Romans, they did let fall their former peacock's bravery and ambition, so that, having fortified themselves with high and strong walls, and furnished the city with all sorts of weapons (offensive and defensive), as likewise with **corn** and all manner of provisions, they cheerfully endured a siege, which, though tedious to them, was no less troublesome and distressing to the besiegers. For the Romans had never been accustomed to stay away from home except in summer, and for no great length of time; and were accustomed to winter at home.

Part Two

And now, the seventh year of the war drawing to an end, the commanders began to be suspected as too slow and remiss in driving on the siege: whereupon in the end they were discharged, and other captains chosen. Among those, Camillus was one, whom then for the second time they created tribune. But at present he had no hand in the siege, the duties that fell by lot to him being to make war upon the **Faliscans** and the **Capenates**. These people, whilst the Romans were occupied elsewhere, had invaded their country, and done them great harm, during the time of their war with the Tuscans; but were now reduced by Camillus, and with great loss shut up within their own walls.

And now, in the very heat of the war, a strange phenomenon in the **Alban lake**, which in the absence of any known cause and explanation by natural reasons, did marvellously amaze the Romans, being no less wonderful than the most strange and uncrediblest thing that could be told by man. It was the beginning of autumn, and the summer now ending had, to all observation, been neither rainy nor much troubled with southern winds; and of the many lakes, brooks, and springs of all sorts with which Italy abounds, some were wholly dried up, others drew very little water with them; all the rivers, as is usual in summer, ran in a very low and hollow channel. But the Alban lake, that is fed by now other waters but its own, and is on all sides encircled with fruitful mountains, without any cause, unless it were divine, began visibly to rise and swell, increasing to the feet of the mountains, and by degrees reaching the level of the very tops of them, and all this without any waves or agitation. At first it was the wonder of shepherds and herdsmen; but when the earth, which, like a great dam, held up the lake from falling into the lower grounds, through the quantity and weight of water was broken down, and in a violent stream it ran through the ploughed fields and plantations to discharge itself in the sea, it not only struck, terror into the Romans, but was thought by all the inhabitants of Italy to **portend** some extraordinary event. But the greatest talk of it was in the camp that besieged Veii, so that in the town itself, also, the occurrence became known.

As in long sieges it commonly happens that parties on both sides meet often and converse with one another; so it chanced that a Roman had gained much confidence and familiarity with one of the besieged, a man versed in ancient prophecies, and of repute for more than ordinary skill in divination. The Roman, observing him to be overjoyed at the story of the lake, and to mock at the siege, told him that this was not the only **prodigy** that of late had happened to the Romans; others more wonderful yet than this had befallen them, which he was willing to communicate to him, that his own private matters might prosper well with him. The man greedily embraced the proposal, expecting to hear some wonderful secrets; but when, by little and little, he had led him on in conversation and insensibly drawn him a good way from the gates of the city, he snatched him up by the middle, being stronger than he, and, by the assistance of others that came running from the camp, seized and delivered him to the commanders.

The Veian seeing himself thus forcibly used, and knowing also that fatal destiny cannot be avoided, began to declare unto the Romans the ancient oracles and prophecies touching the fortune of their city; that it was not possible the city should be taken until the Alban lake, which now broke forth and had found out new passages, was drawn back from that course, and so diverted that it could not mingle with the sea.

This was carried unto the Senate at Rome, to be consulted of in council: and there it was determined they should send to **the oracle of Apollo, at the city of Delphi**, and ask him what they should do therein.

The messengers *[omission for length]*, having made their voyage by sea and consulted the god, returned with the command that the Alban water, if it were possible, they should keep from the sea, and shut it up in its ancient bounds; but if that was not to be done, then they should carry it off by ditches and trenches into lower grounds, and so dry it up; which message being delivered, the priests performed what related to the sacrifices, and the people went to work and turned the water.

Narration and Discussion

If you were a Roman who had never had to pay taxes before, what might your reaction have been to Camillus' new program?

Why was the war against Veii so unpopular with the Romans at the time Camillus became a consular tribune?

Creative narration: You are a Roman school teacher trying to explain how the government works. What questions might the students ask? How would you respond?

For older students and further thought: The story about channeling the water of Lake Albano was important to the Romans, as it lent religious significance to an engineering project, and also emphasized their own cleverness and strength. Are there stories from your own or other cultures that serve a similar purpose?

Lesson Two

Introduction

This lesson shows Camillus at a time of great personal success and acclaim (crushing the city of Veii, triumphing in splendour), but it also shows his frequent struggle against popular opinion, and particularly against rivals who knew how to make use of "mob rule."

Vocabulary

general of horse: second-in-command (see introductory notes)

Matuta, the Mother: a goddess of the Latins

Juno: a major female goddess, wife of Jupiter

entrails: inner organs, believed to be useful for divination

being taken by storm: In this violent event, any Veiians not killed were taken as slaves. It seems pertinent to mention this here because, later on, the Romans considered moving some of their people to Veii, and it helps to understand why the city then stood empty.

Jupiter: the supreme god of the Romans

vouchsafe: promise

felicitations: congratulations, praise

tumultuous: noisy, uproarious

Historic Occasions

396 B.C.: After Rome suffered military defeats against Veii and its allies, Camillus was named dictator and led the capture of the city.

Reading

Part One

And now the Senate, in the tenth year of the war, taking away all other commands, created Camillus dictator; who chose Cornelius Scipio for his **general of horse**. He made vows unto the gods that, if they would grant a happy conclusion of the war, he would celebrate to their honour the great games, and dedicate a temple to the goddess whom the Romans call **Matuta, the Mother** *[omission for content]*.

Camillus then entered with his army into the Faliscan territory, and in a great battle overthrew them and the Capenates, their confederates. From there he went to the siege of Veii, where, perceiving to take it by assault was not to be won without great danger, he proceeded to cut mines underground, the earth about the city being easy to break up and allowing such depth for the works as would prevent their being discovered by the enemy.

This design going on in a hopeful way, he openly gave assaults to the enemy to keep them to the walls, whilst they that worked underground in the mines were, without being perceived, arrived within the citadel, close to the temple of **Juno**, which was the greatest and most honoured in all the city. It is said that the prince of the Tuscans was at that very time at sacrifice; and that the priest, after he had looked into the **entrails** of the beast, cried out with a loud voice that the gods would give the victory to those that should complete those offerings; and that the Romans who were in the mines, hearing the words, immediately pulled down the floor, and, ascending with noise and clashing of weapons, frightened away the enemy, and, snatching up the entrails, carried them to Camillus. But this may look like a fable.

The city, however, **being taken by storm**, and the soldiers busied in pillaging and gathering an infinite quantity of riches and spoils; Camillus, from the high tower viewing what was done, at first wept for pity. And when those that were about him congratulated his success, he lifted up his hands unto heaven, and made this prayer:

> "O mighty god **Jupiter**, and you, O gods, which see and judge men's good and ill works: you know right well that we have not willingly (without wrong and cause offered us) begun this war, but justly, and by compulsion, to be revenged of a city our enemy, which hath done us great injuries. But if to countervail this our great good prosperity, and victory, some bitter adversity and overthrow be predestined unto us: I beseech you then (most merciful gods) in sparing our city of Rome, and this her army, you will (with as little hurt as may be) let it all fall and light upon my person alone."

And as he had spoken these words, and was turning to the right (according to the manner of the Romans after they have prayed unto the gods), he stumbled and fell. The standers-by, taking this for an ill token, were somewhat troubled with the matter; but after he got up on his feet again, he told them that he had received what he had prayed for, a small mischance, in compensation for the greatest good fortune.

Having sacked the city, he was also desirous to carry Juno's image to Rome, to accomplish the vow he had made. And having sent for workmen for this purpose, he did sacrifice first unto the goddess, beseeching her to accept well of the Romans' goodwill, and that she would willingly **vouchsafe** to come and dwell with the other gods who had the protection of the city of Rome *[omission for length and content]*.

Part Two

Now Camillus, whether puffed up with the greatness of his achievement in conquering a city that was the rival of Rome, and had held out a ten years' siege; or exalted with the **felicitations** of those that were about him, assumed to himself more than became a civil and legal magistrate. Among other things, in the pride and haughtiness of his triumph, he was carried through Rome upon his triumphant chariot drawn with four fair white horses, which no general either before or since ever did; for the Romans consider such a mode of conveyance to be sacred, and specially set apart to the king and father of the gods. This bred him much envy amongst the citizens, which had not been acquainted with such pomp and display.

There was another occasion also that made them mislike him much, which was his opposing the law by which the city was to be divided; for the tribunes of the people brought forward a motion that the people and Senate should be divided into two parts, one of which should remain at home, the other, as the lot should decide, remove to the new-taken city. By this means they should not only have much more room, but, by the advantage of two great and magnificent cities, be better able to maintain their territories and their fortunes in general. The people, therefore, who were numerous and indigent, greedily embraced it, and crowded continually to the Forum, with **tumultuous** demands to have it put to the vote. But the Senate and the noblest citizens, judging the proceedings of the tribunes to tend rather to a destruction than a division of Rome, greatly averse to it, went to Camillus for assistance; who, fearing the result if it came to a direct contest, contrived to occupy the people with other business, and so staved it off. He thus became unpopular with the common people.

Narration and Discussion

Why did it seem significant that Camillus stumbled? How did he explain it?

Creative narration: You are a Roman reporter who has heard that Camillus is "unpopular with the common people." Interview various people to find out why.

Lesson Three

Introduction

After the taking of Veii, there was a logistical problem: some of the treasure had been promised as a gift in gratitude to the gods, but the actual pieces had already been sold, and the money spent. Replacement gold was collected, with more enthusiasm by some (the Roman women) than others (the soldiers); and, after many adventures, it was deposited at a temple in Delphi.

And soon afterwards, the city of Falerii was taken by the Romans, though in a very different manner than that of Veii.

Vocabulary

the tenth part of their spoils: that is, of the loot taken from the capture of Veii

he was discharged of his charge: he stepped down as dictator

levied: collected

massy: usually refers to weight ("massive", bulky); can also mean unalloyed or pure; the best translation would probably be "solid gold," which includes both meanings.

sent to Delphi: that is, to the temple there

talent: A talent of gold is estimated to have weighed 110 lb. (50 kg).

recompense: reward

obsequies: funeral rites

rovers: pirates

division of the city: see previous lesson

ratified: approved, given consent

Historic Occasions

394 B.C.: Camillus was appointed consular tribune to lead the final campaign against the Faliscans (and their city of Falerii)

On the Map

Lipari (Liparians): the largest of the **Aeolian Islands**, off the northern coast of Sicily

Reading

Part One

But the original and apparent cause of the people's ill will towards Camillus was for taking from them **the tenth part of their spoils**: and his taking of it was not altogether without some reason, and to say truly the people did him much wrong to bear him such malice for that. For before he went to Veii, he made a solemn vow to offer the tenth part unto the gods, of the spoils of the city, if he won the same. But when it was taken and sacked, whether it was that he was loath to trouble the citizens, or having a world of business in his head, that he easily forgot his vow: he suffered the soldiers to divide the spoil amongst them, and to take the benefit to themselves.

Shortly after **he was discharged of his charge**, he did inform the Senate of his vow. Furthermore, the soothsayers made report at that very time, how they knew by certain signs and tokens of their sacrifices, that the gods were offended for something, and how they must of necessity be pacified again. Whereupon the Senate presently made an order, where it was impossible every man should bring in again the selfsame things he had gotten, to make a new division of every man's share: that everyone therefore, upon his oath, should present the tenth part of his gains he had gotten by that booty.

This occasioned many annoyances and hardships to the soldiers, who were poor men, and had endured much in the war, and now were forced, out of what they had gained and spent, to bring in so great a proportion; and for this trouble, they all cried out with open mouth against Camillus. For want of a better excuse, he betook himself to the poorest of defenses, saying that, forsooth, he had forgotten his vow. They in turn complained that he had vowed the tenth of the enemy's goods, and now **levied** it out of the tenth of the citizens'.

Nevertheless, everyone having brought in his due proportion, it was decreed that out of it a bowl of **massy** gold should be made, and **sent to Delphi**. And when there was great scarcity of gold in the city, and the magistrates were considering where to get it, the Roman ladies, meeting together and consulting among themselves, out of the golden ornaments they wore they contributed as much as went to the making of the offering, which in weight came to eight **talents** of gold. In **recompense** whereof, to honour them withal: the Senate ordained that they should be praised openly with funeral orations at their burial, as they did use at honourable and noble men's **obsequies**. For before that law, it was not the manner to praise women openly at their funerals.

Part Two

Now there were appointed three of the noblest men of the city to go to carry this offering, and they sent them out in a galley well manned, stored also with good mariners, and trimly set forth in all triumphing manner: howbeit both in storm, and calm weather, they were in danger of their lives. For after that they had escaped drowning very narrowly by tempest, when the wind was down again, they fell into another danger, which they escaped also beyond all hope. For hard by the **Aeolian Islands**, the galleys of the **Liparians** fell upon them, as if they had been **rovers**. But when the Liparians saw they made no resistance, and entreated them, holding up their hands: they gave no further charge upon them, but only fastened their galley unto theirs.

So when they had hauled them to the shore, where they expected to sell their goods and persons as lawful prize, they being pirates; and scarcely, at last, by the virtue and interest of one man, Timasitheus by name, who was in office as general, and used his utmost persuasion, they were, with much ado, dismissed. He, however, himself sent out some of his own vessels with them, to accompany them in their voyage and assist them at the dedication; for which he received honours at Rome, according to his well deserving.

Part Three

The tribunes of the people again resuming their motion for the **division of the city**, the war against the Faliscans luckily broke out, giving liberty to the chief citizens to choose what magistrates they pleased, and to appoint Camillus military tribune, with five colleagues; affairs then requiring a commander of authority and reputation, as well as experience. And when the people had **ratified** the election, he marched with his forces into the territories of the Faliscans, and laid siege to Falerii, a well-fortified city, and plentifully stored with all necessaries of war *[omission for length]*.

But the Falerians trusting in the situation of their city, which was very strong in all parts, made so little account of the siege that those which kept not watch upon the walls, walked up and down in their gowns in the city, without any weapon about them; and their children went to school. The schoolmaster also would commonly lead them abroad out of the city a-walking, to play and pass the time by the town walls. For the Falerians, like the Greeks, used to have a single teacher for many pupils, wishing their children to live and be brought up from the beginning in each other's company.

This schoolmaster, designing to betray the Falerians by their children, led them out every day under the town wall, at first but a little way, and, when they had exercised, brought them home again. Afterwards by degrees he drew them farther and farther, till by practice he had made them bold and fearless, as if no danger was about them.

But at the length, one day having gotten all the citizens' children with him, he led them within the watch of the Romans' camp, and there delivered all his scholars into their hands, and prayed them they would bring him unto their general. So they did. And when he came before Camillus, he began to tell him that he was schoolmaster unto all these children, nevertheless that he did more esteem to have his grace and favour, than regard his office he had by this name and title.

Camillus hearing what he said, and beholding his treacherous part, he said to those that were about him:

> "War of itself surely is an evil thing, for in wars many injuries and mischiefs are done: nevertheless among good men there is a law and discipline, which doth forbid them to seek victory by wicked and traitorous means, and that a noble and worthy general should make war, and procure victory, by trusting to his own valiantness, and not by another's vileness and villainy."

Therefore he commanded his sergeants to bind his hands behind him *[omission for content]*: and that they should give the children rods and whips in their hands, to whip the traitor back again into the city, that had thus betrayed them, and grieved their parents.

Now when the Falerians heard news that the schoolmaster had thus betrayed them, all the city fell a-weeping (as every man may think for so great a loss) and men and women ran together one in another's neck, to the town walls, and gates of the city, like people out of their wits, they were so troubled. When they came thither, they saw their children bringing their schoolmaster back again *[omission for content]*, whipping of him, and calling Camillus their father, their god, and their saviour: so that not only the fathers and mothers of the children, but all the citizens, did conceive in themselves a wonderful admiration and great love of the wisdom, goodness, and justice of Camillus.

Narration and Discussion

How did Camillus create a very different impression in his treatment of the Falerians vs. his actions in Veii? What might have been the reasons for this?

For older students: "Among good men there is a law and discipline, which doth forbid them to seek victory by wicked and traitorous means…": do you agree? Do you think Camillus will be able to maintain this philosophy?

Creative narration: Retell either the story of the collection and journey with the gold, or the story of the traitorous teacher, in any creative format you like (drama, artwork, comic strip, song).

Lesson Four

Introduction

In 391 B.C., sulking soldiers and stubborn city-dividers successfully managed to impeach Camillus. Refusing to pay his fine (or to accept its payment by others), he went into exile in the city of Ardea.

The second half of the lesson introduces a new threat to Rome itself: the Gauls. That story continues through **Lesson Eight**.

Vocabulary

resign whatever they had to his disposal: give up their rights and property to him

making a peace with the whole nation of the Faliscans, returned home: Plutarch moves on quickly to other matters, but it is worth noting that as a result of this victory, other city-states such as Aequi, Volsci, and Capena proposed peace treaties with Rome. Rome now controlled a much larger territory and was the strongest power in that part of Italy.

railed against: criticized

inveighing: speaking negatively, protesting

commiseration: sympathy

abate their malice: let go of their anger

immoderate: great

preferred: proposed, created

appropriation: theft

exasperated: annoyed, out of patience

defamed: slandered, having his reputation damaged

ignominy: public disgrace

choler: anger

like Achilles: in Homer's *Iliad*

imprecations: curses

noised: spread (like news)

People

Gauls: see introductory notes for this study.

Historic Occasions

391 B.C.: Impeachment and exile of Camillus

On the Map

Riphean Mountains: a northern mountain range, of uncertain location

Reading

Part One

Immediately meeting in assembly, the Falerians sent ambassadors to him, to **resign whatever they had to his disposal**. Camillus sent them to Rome, where, being brought into the Senate, they spoke to this purpose: that the Romans, preferring justice before victory, had taught them rather to embrace submission than liberty; they did not so much confess themselves to be inferior in strength, as they must acknowledge the Romans to be superior in virtue. The Senate dispatched letters unto Camillus, to judge and order as he thought fit; who, taking a sum of money of the Falerians, and, **making a peace with the whole nation of the Faliscans, returned home**.

But the soldiers, who had expected to have the pillage of the city, when they came to Rome empty-handed, **railed against** Camillus among their fellow-citizens, saying that he loved not the common people, and how for spite he disappointed their army of the spoil. Afterwards, when the tribunes of the people again brought their motion for dividing the city to the vote, Camillus appeared openly against it, shrinking from no unpopularity, and **inveighing** boldly against the promotors of it, and so urging and constraining the multitude that, contrary to their inclinations, they rejected the proposal, but yet hated Camillus. Insomuch that, though a great misfortune befell him in his family (one of his two sons dying of a disease), **commiseration** for this could not in the least make them **abate their malice**. And, indeed, he took this loss with **immoderate** sorrow, being a man naturally of a mild and tender disposition; and, when the accusation was **preferred** against him, he kept his house, and mourned amongst the women of his family.

The accuser was Lucius Apuleius (a tribune of the people); the charge, **appropriation** of the Tuscan spoils; certain brass gates, part of those spoils, were said to be in his (Camillus') possession. The people were **exasperated** against him, and it was plain they would take hold of any occasion to condemn him. Wherefore calling together his friends and soldiers that had served under him in the wars, or that had taken charge with him, which were many in number: he earnestly besought them, that they would not suffer him thus vilely to be condemned, through false and unjust accusations laid against him, nor to be so scorned and **defamed** by his enemies. His friends having laid their heads together, and consulted thereupon, made him answer: how for his judgment they could not remedy it, but if he were condemned, they would all join together, with a very goodwill, to help to pay his fine. But he being of mind not to bear such an open shame and **ignominy**, determined in **choler** to leave the city, and to exile himself from it.

And after he had taken his leave of his wife and children, bidding them farewell: he went out of his house to the gates of the city, and said never a word. When he came thither, he stayed suddenly, and returning back again, he lift up his hands towards the Capitol, and made his prayers unto the gods: that if it were of very spite and malice, and not of just deserving, that the common people compelled him thus shamefully to forsake the city, that the Romans might quickly repent them, and in the face of the world might wish for him, and have need of him.

Thus, **like Achilles**, having left his **imprecations** on the citizens, he went into banishment; so that, neither appearing nor making defense, he was condemned in the sum of a great deal of money. And there is not a Roman but believes that immediately upon the prayers of Camillus, a sudden judgment followed, and that he received a revenge for the injustice done unto him; which though we cannot think was pleasant, but rather grievous and bitter to him, yet was very remarkable, and **noised** over the whole world.

Part Two

Such a punishment visited the city of Rome: an era of such loss and danger and disgrace so quickly succeeded, whether it thus fell out by Fortune, or it be the office of some god not to see injured virtue go unavenged.

Their first token that threatened some great mischief to light upon them, was the death of Julius, one of the censors: for the Romans do greatly reverence the office of a censor, and esteem it as a sacred place.

The second token that happened a little before Camillus' exile, was this: that one Marcus Caeditius, a man but of mean quality, and none of the senators (but otherwise a fair conditioned honest man, and of good conscience) told the military tribunes of a thing that was to be well considered of. For he said that the night before, as he was going on his way in the street called the New Way, he heard someone call him aloud: and returning back to see what it was, he saw no living creature, but only heard a voice bigger than a man's, which said unto him: "Marcus Caeditius, go thy way tomorrow morning to the military tribunes and bid them look quickly for the **Gauls**."

The tribunes were merry at the matter, and made but a jest at his warning; and, straight after that came the condemnation of Camillus.

A Sidebar About the Gauls

Now as touching the Gauls. They came (as they say) of the Celts, whose country not being able to maintain the multitudes of them, they were driven to go seek other countries to inhabit: and there were amongst them many thousands of young men of service and good soldiers, but yet more women and little children by a great number.

Of these people, some of them went towards the north sea, passing the **Riphean Mountains**, and did dwell in the extreme parts of Europe. Other of them remained between the Pyrenees, and the greatest mountains of the Alps, near unto the Senones, and the Celtorii. There they continued a long time, until they fortuned in the end to taste of the wine, which was first brought out of Italy unto them. Which drink they found so good, and were so delighted with it, that suddenly they armed themselves: and taking their wives and children with them, they went directly towards the Alps, to go seek out the country that brought forth such fruit, judging all other countries, in respect of that, to be but wild and barren *[omission for length and content]*.

So they conquered at their first coming all that country which the Tuscans held in old time, reaching from the Alps to both the seas, as the names themselves testify: for the north or Adriatic Sea is named from the Tuscan city, Adria; and that to the south simply the Tuscan Sea. All that country is well planted with trees, and hath goodly pleasant pastures for beasts and cattle to feed in, and is notably watered with goodly running rivers. It had eighteen large and beautiful cities, well provided with all the means for industry and wealth, and all the enjoyments and pleasures of life. The Gauls cast out the Tuscans, and seated themselves in them. (But this was long before.)

Narration and Discussion

Why were the soldiers disappointed about the lack of violence in the taking of Falerii? How did this contribute towards the general desire to discredit Camillus?

Why did Camillus choose exile over a compromise that would have allowed him to stay in Rome?

What impressions do you have of the Gauls?

Creative narration: The somewhat similar events of *Coriolanus* inspired Shakespeare to write a play around them. Write a scene where people discuss recent misfortunes in Rome, and worry about what else could go wrong. Older students could also write a soliloquy for Camillus, expressing his feelings at this time.

Lesson Five

Introduction

The Gauls, politely asked by the Romans not to invade cities that had caused them no injury, laughed in their faces and pointed out that they, the Romans, had done exactly that to others.

Then they, incredibly, scored such a victory over the Romans (at the Battle of the River Allia) that they themselves were surprised to enter the city (in **Lesson Six**) and find it almost emptied.

Vocabulary

barbarous: At its most negative, "barbarous" or "barbaric" means brutal and cruel, which might be an accurate description of the Gauls. It may also simply mean uncivilized and primitive (at least from the Roman perspective).

giving over: ceasing

glistering: shining

skirmishing: fighting small battles

priests called the *Faeciales*: Plutarch explains that these priests were considered the guardians of peace, and "the judges of all causes by which war might justifiably be made."

done the fact: committed the crime

dissolute: unfaithful, lax

stole by night to Veii: The survivors of the battle went to the deserted city of Veii; many of the Roman civilians, taking advantage of the Gauls' leisurely pace, escaped to the Etruscan city of Caere; but a remaining garrison held out on the Capitoline Hill. According to

Plutarch, though, Rome was not entirely deserted, because we later read that the Gauls, entering the city, killed all those they found.

People

Brennus, King of the Gauls: or Chief of the Senones, a tribe which battled the Romans until 283 B.C., when they were finally defeated

Historic Occasions

c. 391 B.C.: Siege of Clusium

July 390 B.C.: Gauls marched towards Rome, defeated Rome at the Battle of the Allia, and seized the city

On the Map

Clusium (Clusinians): a city in Tuscany (present-day Chiusi)

River Allia: a small river in Lazio, and a tributary of the **Tiber**, which flows through Rome

Reading

Part One

Now the Gauls, being further entered into Tuscany, did besiege the city of **Clusium**. Thereupon the Clusinians seeking aid of the Romans, besought them they would send letters and ambassadors unto these **barbarous** people in their favour. They sent unto them three of the best and most honourable persons of the city, all three of the house of the Fabians. The Gauls received them very courteously, from respect to the name of Rome; and, **giving over** the assault which was then making upon the walls, came to conference with them. When the ambassadors asked what injury they had received of the Clusinians that they thus invaded their city, **Brennus, King of the Gauls**, laughed and made answer:

"The Clusians do us injury in that, being able only to

> till a small parcel of ground, they must needs possess a great territory, and will not yield any part to us who are strangers, many in number, and poor. The like wrong was offered unto you Romans in old time, by those of Alba, by the Fidenates, and the Ardeates; and not long since, by the Veians, and the Capenates; and partly by the Falisces and the Volsces, against whom ye have taken, and do take arms, at all times. And as oft as they will let ye have no part of their goods, ye imprison their persons, rob and spoil their goods, and destroy their cities. And in doing this, ye do them no wrong at all, but follow the oldest law that is in the world, whichever leaveth unto the stronger, that which the weaker cannot keep and enjoy. Beginning with the gods, and ending with beasts: the which have this property in nature, that the bigger and stronger have ever the advantage of the weaker and lesser. Therefore, leave your pity to see the Clusians besieged, lest you teach us Gauls to take compassion also of those you have oppressed."

By this answer the Romans, perceiving that Brennus was not to be treated with, went into Clusium, and encouraged and stirred up the inhabitants to make a sally with them upon the barbarians, which they did either to try their strength or to show their own.

The sally being made, and the fight growing hot about the walls, one of the Fabii, Quintus Ambustus, being well mounted, and setting spurs to his horse, made full against a Gaul, a man of huge bulk and stature, whom he saw riding out at a distance from the rest. He (Quintus Ambustus) was not recognized, as his **glistering** armour dimmed the eyes of the enemies.

But after he had slain the Gaul, and came to strip him: Brennus then knew him, and protested against him, calling the gods to witness how he had broken the law of arms: that, coming as an ambassador, he had taken upon him the form of an enemy. Hereupon Brennus forthwith left **skirmishing**, and raising the siege from Clusium, led his army directly to Rome.

But not wishing that it should look as if they took advantage of that injury, and were ready to embrace any occasion offered, he sent a herald to demand the man in punishment, that he might punish him accordingly; and in the meantime marched leisurely on to receive their answer.

Part Two

The Senate hereupon assembled, and many of the senators blamed the rashness of the Fabians. The **priests called the *Faeciales*** were the most decided: on religious grounds, they urged the Senate that they should lay the whole weight and burden of it upon him alone, that only had **done the fact**. The Senate referred the whole matter to the people; and the priests there, as well as in the Senate, were against the Fabians; the multitude, however, so little regarded their authority, that instead of delivering Quintus Ambustus unto the enemy, they did choose him for one of the military tribunes, along with his brothers.

The Gauls, on hearing this, in great rage threw aside every delay, and hastened on with all the speed they could make. The places through which they marched, terrified with their numbers and the splendour of their preparations for war, and in alarm at their violence and fierceness, began to give up their territories as already lost, with little doubt but their cities would quickly follow. Contrary, however, to expectation, the Gauls did no injury as they passed, nor took anything from the fields; and, as they went by any city, cried out that they went to Rome, and would have no wars but with the Romans, and how otherwise they desired to be friends with all the world.

These barbarous people marching on in this wise towards Rome, the military tribunes brought their army to the field to encounter them. They were no less in number than the Gauls, for they were forty thousand footmen. Howbeit most part of them were raw soldiers, and such as never handled a weapon before. Besides, they were very careless of the gods, and **dissolute** in matters of religion: for they passed neither for good signs in their sacrifices, neither to ask counsel of their soothsayers, which the Romans were religiously wont to do, before they gave any battle. To make the matter worse, the number of the captains having power and authority alike, did as much (or more than the rest) disorder and confound their doings. Frequently before, upon lesser occasions, they had chosen a single leader, with the title of dictator, being sensible of what great importance it is in critical times to have the soldiers united under one general with the entire and absolute control placed in his hands. The injury also which they had to ungratefully done to Camillus, brought great mischief and inconvenience then upon them. For the captains after him dared no more command the people roughly, but ever after did flatter them much.

In this condition they left the city, and encamped by the **River Allia**, about ten miles from Rome, and not far from the place where it falls into the **Tiber**; and here the Gauls came upon them, and, after a disgraceful resistance, devoid of order and discipline, they were miserably defeated. The left wing was immediately driven into the river, and there destroyed; the right had less damage by declining the shock, and from the low grounds getting to the tops of the hills, from whence most of them afterwards dropped into the city; the rest, as many as escaped the enemy being weary of the slaughter, **stole by night to Veii,** giving up Rome and all that was in it for lost.

[Omission for length]

Narration and Discussion

Describe Brennus from a Roman point of view. How might someone of his own tribe describe him differently?

Explain this sentence: "For the captains after [Camillus] dared no more command the people roughly, but ever after did flatter them much."

Creative narration: Write Camillus a letter, informing him of what has been going on around Rome.

Lesson Six

Introduction

The Romans, after the shock of seeing their own city burned, and hearing of the brutal murder of their elders, agreed that they needed the leadership of Camillus. But would he be willing to help?

Vocabulary

leisure: opportunity, time

works: fortifications

vestal virgins: Vesta was the goddess of hearth and home, and the vestal virgins were young women responsible for maintaining her sacred fire. (North translates it "nuns.")

devoting: committing a thing or a person to God or the gods

design or stratagem: plot, trick

razed: destroyed, burned down

in want of provision: short of food

sojourned: stayed, lived

enterprise: boldness, resolve

mustered: gathered (to fight)

Historic Occasions

390 B.C.: Rome was occupied by the Gauls

On the Map

Ardea: a town of the Lazio region, 22 miles (35 km) south of Rome (it is now within the Metropolitan City of Rome)

Reading

Part One

Now after this battle lost, if the Gauls had hotly pursued the chase of their flying enemies, nothing could have saved Rome from being taken, and the inhabitants thereof from being put unto the sword; such was the terror that those who escaped the battle brought with them into the city, and with such distraction and confusion were themselves in turn infected. But the Gauls, not imagining their victory to be so considerable, and overtaken with the present joy, fell to feasting and dividing the spoil; by which means they gave **leisure** to those who were for leaving the city to make their escape, and to those that remained to anticipate and prepare for their coming.

For they who resolved to stay at Rome, abandoning the rest of the city, betook themselves to the Capitol, which they fortified with the help of missiles and new **works**. One of their principal cares was of their holy things, most of which they conveyed into the Capitol.

A sidebar about sacred things

But the consecrated fire, the **vestal virgins** took and fled with it, as likewise their other sacred things.

[Omission for length; it is unclear exactly what they took with them.]

However it be, taking the most precious and important things they had, they fled away with them, shaping their course along the riverside, where Lucius Albinius, a simple citizen of Rome, who among others was making his escape, overtook them, having his wife, children, and goods in a cart; and, seeing the virgins, dragging along in their arms the holy things of the gods, in a helpless and weary condition, he caused his wife and children to get down, and, taking out his goods, put the virgins in the cart, that they might make their escape to some of the Greek cities. This devout act of Albinius, and the respect he showed thus signally to the gods at a time of such extremity, deserved not to be passed over in silence.

Part Two

But the priests that belonged to other gods, and the most elderly of the senators, men who had been consuls and had enjoyed triumphs, could not endure to leave the city; but, putting on their sacred and splendid robes, Fabius the high priest performing the office, they made their prayers to the gods, and, **devoting** themselves, as it were, for their country, sat themselves down in their ivory chairs in the Forum, and in that posture expected the event.

On the third day after the battle, Brennus came to Rome with his army: who, finding the gates of the city all open, and the walls without watch, he first began to suspect it was some **design or stratagem**, never dreaming that the Romans were in so desperate a condition. But when he found it to be so indeed, he entered at the Colline gate, and took Rome, in the three hundred and sixtieth year, or a little more, after it was built *[omission for length]*. After taking possession of Rome, he set a strong guard about the Capitol; and, going down into the Forum, was there struck with amazement at the sight of so many men sitting in that order and silence, observing that they neither rose at his coming, not so much as changed colour or countenance, but remained without fear or concern, leaning upon their staves, and sitting quietly, looking at each other. This their so strange manner at the first did so damp the Gauls, that for a space they stood still, and were in doubt to come near to touch them, fearing lest they had been some gods: until such time, as one of them went boldly unto Marcus Papirius, and laid his hand fair and softly upon his long beard. But Papirius gave him such a rap on his head with his staff, that he made the blood run about his ears. This barbarous beast was in such a rage with the blow, that he drew out his sword, and slew him.

The other soldiers also killed all the rest afterwards: and so the Gauls continued many days spoiling and sacking all things they found in the houses, and in the end did set them all afire, and destroyed them every one, for despite of those that guarded the Capitol, that would not yield upon their summons, but valiantly repulsed them when they scaled the walls. For this cause they **razed** the whole city, and put all to the sword that came in their hands, young and old, man, woman, and child.

Part Three

And now, the siege of the Capitol having lasted a good while, the Gauls began to be **in want of provision**; and, dividing their forces, part of them stayed with their kind at the siege, the rest went to forage the country, ravaging the towns and villages where they came, but not all together in a body, but in different squadrons and parties; and to such a confidence had success raised them, that they carelessly rambled about without the least fear or apprehension of danger.

But the greatest and best-ordered body of their forces went to the city of **Ardea**, where Camillus then **sojourned**, having, ever since his leaving Rome, meddling with no matters of state from the time of his exile until that present time; but now he began to rouse up himself, and consider not how to avoid or escape the enemy, but to find out an opportunity to be revenged upon them. And perceiving that the Ardeatians wanted not men, but rather **enterprise**, through the inexperience and timidity of their officers, he began to speak with the young men, saying that:

> they ought not to ascribe the misfortune of the Romans to the courage of their enemy, nor attribute the losses they sustained by rash counsel to the conduct of men who had no title to victory; the event had been only an evidence of the power of fortune; that it was a brave thing even with danger to repel a foreign and barbarous invader whose end in conquering was but to destroy and consume, as fire, all that fell into their hands. Wherefore if they would but only take a good lusty heart and courage unto them, he would with opportunity, and place, assure them the victory, without any danger.

When Camillus found the young men embraced the idea, he went to the magistrates and council of Ardea, and, having persuaded them also, he **mustered** all that could bear arms.

Narration and Discussion

Do you agree that the elders of Rome showed great courage? (Should they have armed themselves for battle instead?)

Which is more surprising: that the Romans asked Camillus to lead a counterattack against the Gauls, or that he agreed to help them?

For further thought: Those who have read *Coriolanus* may want to compare his actions with those of Camillus. How did they differ?

Creative narration: Those who found the earlier Shakespeare-inspired exercise interesting might add to it in this lesson. Which events would you portray onstage, and which would you have other characters describe? How might Shakespeare have rewritten Camillus' speech?

Lesson Seven

Introduction

The plan to retake Rome involved surrounding the city, and then deciding how and when to attack. Camillus, insistent on doing things by the book, delayed taking on the office of dictator (or general) until it had been properly ratified by the Roman senators, who were besieged on the Capitoline Hill. But how would they get that request past the Gauls?

In the second part of the reading, the Gauls followed the path of that messenger to scale the hill and attack the garrison; however, their attempts at stealth were foiled by some patriotic geese.

Vocabulary

the ground that lay between: between Ardea and the enemy camp

works: fortifications

be their captain: Camillus was being offered an unofficial generalship.

the victory of Camillus: the taking of the camp

make them privy to it: inform them of it

invincible: unconquerable

their just desert: what they deserve

rampart: defensive wall

People

Pontius Cominius: also called Cominius Pontius

Marcus Manlius, later called Capitolinus: consul in 392 B.C.; tribune in 389 B.C. He was the brother of Aulius Manlius Capitolinus, a consular tribune.

Historic Occasions

390 B.C.: Camillus named dictator for the second time

Reading

Part One

Camillus drew his soldiers up within the walls of Ardea, that they might not be perceived by the enemy, who was near; who, having scoured the country, and now returned heavy-laden with spoils, lay encamped in the plains in a careless and negligent posture; and having their full carriage of wine, laid them down to sleep, and made no noise at all in their camp.

When Camillus learned this from his scouts, he drew out the Ardeatians, and in the dead of the night, passing in silence over **the ground that lay between**, came up to their **works**, and, commanding his trumpets to sound and his men to shout and halloo, he struck terror into them from all quarters; who yet with all the loud noise they made, could hardly be made to wake, they were so deadly drunk. A few, whom fear had sobered, getting into some order, for a while resisted; and so died with their weapons in their hands. But the greatest part of them, buried in wine and sleep, were surprised without their arms, and put to death; and as many of them as by the advantage of the night got out of the camp were the next day found scattered abroad and wandering in the fields, and were picked up by the horsemen which followed and killed them, as they took them straggling here and there in the fields.

The fame of this action soon flew through the neighbouring cities, and stirred up the young men from various quarters to come and join themselves with him. But none were so much concerned as those Romans who escaped in the Battle of Allia, and were now at Veii, thus lamenting with themselves,

"O gods, what a captain hath fortune taken from the

> city of Rome? What honour hath the city of Ardea by the valiantness and worthy deeds of Camillus; and in the mean season, his natural city that brought him forth, is now lost and utterly destroyed? We, for lack of a captain to lead us, are shut up here within others' walls, and do nothing but suffer Italy in the mean space to go to ruin, and utter destruction before our eyes. Why then do we not send to the Ardeans for our captain, or why do we not arm ourselves, to go unto him? For he is now no more a banished man, nor we poor citizens: since our city is possessed with the foreign power of our hateful enemies."

So they all agreed to this counsel, and sent unto Camillus, to beseech him to **be their captain** and lead them. But he made answer, he would in no case consent unto it, unless they that were besieged in the Capitol had lawfully first confirmed it by their voices. "For those," (said he) "so long as they remain within the city, do represent the state and body thereof." Therefore if they commanded him to take this charge upon him, he would most willingly obey them: if otherwise they misliked of it, that then he would not meddle against their goodwills and commandment.

They having received this answer, there was not a Roman amongst them but greatly honoured and extolled the wisdom and justice of Camillus. But now they knew not how to **make them privy to it**, that were besieged in the Capitol: for they saw no possibility to convey a messenger to them: considering the enemies were lords of the city, and laid siege to it. Howbeit there was one **Pontius Cominius** amongst the young men (a man of a mean house, but yet desirous of honour and glory) that offered himself very willingly to venture to get in if he could.

So he took no letters to carry to them which were besieged, for fear lest they might be intercepted, and so they should discover Camillus' intention; but putting on a poor dress and carrying corks under it, he boldly travelled the greatest part of the way by day, and came to the city when it was dark. The bridge he could not pass, as it was guarded by the barbarians; so that taking his clothes, which were neither many nor heavy, and binding them about his head, he laid his body upon the corks, and swimming with them, got over to the city. Avoiding those quarters where he perceived the enemy was awake, he went to the Carmental gate, where there was greatest silence, and where the hill of the Capitol is steepest and rises with craggy and broken rock. By this way he got up, though with much difficulty, by the hollow of the cliff, and presented himself to the guards, saluting them, and telling them his name; he was taken in and carried to the commanders.

A meeting of the Senate being immediately called, he related to them in order **the victory of Camillus**, which they had not heard of before, and the proceeding of the soldiers, urging them to confirm Camillus in the command, as on him alone all their fellow-countrymen outside the city would rely. Having heard and consulted of the matter, the Senate declared Camillus dictator, and sent back Pontius the same way that he came; who, with the same success as before, got through the enemy without being discovered, and delivered to the Romans outside the decision of the Senate, who joyfully received it. Camillus, on his arrival, found twenty thousand of them ready in arms; with which forces, and those confederates he brought along with him, he prepared to set upon the enemy.

Part Two

But at Rome some of the barbarians, walking out by chance near the place at which Pontius by night had got into the Capitol, spied in several places marks of feet and hands, where he had laid hold and clambered, and places where the plants that grew to the rock had been rubbed off, and the earth had slipped, and went accordingly and reported it to the king, who, coming in person, and viewing it, for the present said nothing, but in the evening, picking out such of the Gauls as were nimblest of body, and by living in the mountains were accustomed to climb, he said to them,

> "The enemy themselves have shown us a way how to come at them, which we could not have found out but by themselves. For they having gone up before us, do give us easily to understand, it is no impossible thing for us to climb up also. Wherefore, we were utterly shamed, having already begun well, if we should fail also to end well: and to leave this

> place as **invincible**. For if it were easy for one man alone, by digging to climb up to the height thereof: much less is it hard for many to get up one after another, so that one do help another. Therefore, Sirs, I assure you, those that do take pains to get up, shall be honourably rewarded, according to **their just desert**."

When the king had spoken these words unto the Gauls, they fell to it lustily every man to get up: and about midnight, they began many of them to dig, and make steps up to the rock one after another, as softly as could possibly, with catching hold the best they could, by the hanging of the rock, which they found very steep, but nevertheless easier to climb, then they took it at the beginning. So that the foremost of them being come to the top of the rock, were now ready to take the wall, and to set upon the watch that slept: for there was neither man nor dog that heard them.

It chanced then there were holy geese kept in the Temple of Juno, which at other times were plentifully fed, but now, by reason that corn and other provisions were grown scarce for all, were but in a poor condition. The creature is by nature of quick sense, and apprehensive of the least noise, so that these, being moreover watchful through hunger, and restless, immediately discovered the coming of the Gauls, and, running up and down with their noise and cackling, they raised the whole camp, while the barbarians on the other side, perceiving themselves discovered, no longer endeavoured to conceal their attempt, and came in with all the open noise and terror they could.

The Romans, everyone in haste snatching up the next weapon that came to hand, did what they could on the sudden occasion. **Marcus Manlius**, a man of consular dignity, of strong body and great spirit, was the first that made head against them, and, engaging with two of the enemy at once, with his sword cut off the right arm of one just as he was lifting up his blade to strike; and, running his target full in the face of the other, tumbled him headlong down the steep rock; then mounting the **rampart**, and there standing with others that came running to his assistance, drove down the rest of them, who, indeed, to begin, had not been many, and did nothing worthy of so bold an attempt. The Romans, having thus escaped this danger, early in the morning took the captain of the watch and flung him down the rock upon the heads of their enemies; and to Manlius for his victory voted a reward, intended more for honour than advantage, bringing him, each man of them, as much as he received for his daily allowance, which was half a pound of bread and one eighth of a pint of wine.

Narration and Discussion

Some of the Romans might have felt that Camillus was wasting time, and perhaps endangering their mission, by worrying about legal procedure. Do you agree with his decision?

Why was the reward for Manlius "more for honour than advantage?"

Creative narration: Tell the story of Pontius Cominius in any creative way you wish. Older students may feel inspired by Macaulay's poem "Horatius at the Bridge," which describes an earlier attempt to save Rome from Etruscan invaders.

Lesson Eight

Introduction

The Roman senators, starving and short on ideas, were finally brought to the point of simply paying the Gauls to leave; and the Gauls, by this point, were equally satisfied to accept this persuasion. However, the weighing out of the gold was interrupted by the arrival of Camillus.

Vocabulary

they wanted provisions: they lacked food

despondency: low spirits, loss of hope

parley: communication, discussion

passing by and dissembling a petty injury: ignoring a small insult

hot: angry

required ought: wanted to transact any business

mad as a march hare: a phrase used as early as 1500 A.D. to describe excitable and unpredictable behaviour; a more current way to describe Brennus' reaction might be to say that he "lost it."

***Aius Locutius*:** Dryden translates the god's name as "Rumour, or Voice;" the words mean "spoken affirmation," referring to the fact that the deity spoke clearly but was known by its voice alone.

Historic Occasions

February 389 B.C.: Rome liberated from the Gauls

Reading

Henceforward, the affairs of the Gauls were daily in a worse and worse condition: **they wanted provisions**, being withheld from foraging (through fear of Camillus); and sickness also was amongst them, occasioned by the number of carcasses that lay in heaps unburied; and amongst burnt houses destroyed, where the ashes being blown very high by the wind and vehemence of heat, breathed up, so to say, a dry and searching air, the inhalation of which was destructive to their health. But the chief cause was the change from their natural climate, coming as they did out of shady and hilly countries, abounding in means of shelter from the heat, to lodge in low, and, in the autumn season, very unhealthy ground; added to which was the length and tediousness of the siege, as they had now sat seven months before the Capitol. There was, therefore, a great destruction among them, and the number of the dead grew so great that the living gave up burying them. Neither, indeed, were things on that account any better with the besieged, for famine increased upon them, and also **despondency** with not hearing anything of Camillus, it being impossible to send any one to him, the city was so guarded by the barbarians.

Things being in this sad condition on both sides, a motion of treaty was made at first by some of the outposts, as they happened to speak with one another; which being embraced by the leading men, Sulpicius, tribune of the Romans, came to a **parley** with Brennus, in which it was agreed that, the Romans laying down a thousand weight of gold, the

Gauls, upon the receipt of it, should immediately depart out of their city, and all their territories.

The agreement being confirmed by oath on both sides, and the gold brought forth, the Gauls used false dealing in the weights, secretly at first, but afterwards openly pulled back and disturbed the balance; at which the Romans indignantly complaining, Brennus, in a scoffing and insulting manner, pulled off his sword and belt, and threw them both into the scales; and when Sulpicius asked what that meant, "What should it mean," says he, "but woe to the conquered?" This word ever after ran as a common proverb in the people's mouths.

And as for the Romans, some were so incensed that they were for taking their gold back again and returning to endure the siege. Others were for **passing by and dissembling a petty injury**, and not to account that the indignity of the thing lay in paying more than was due, since paying anything at all was itself a dishonour only submitted to as a necessity of the times.

Whilst this difference remained still unsettled, both amongst themselves and with the Gauls, Camillus was at the gates with his army. Having learned what was going on, he commanded the main body of his forces to follow slowly after him in good order; and himself with the choicest of his men hastening on, went at once to the Romans; where all giving way to him, and receiving him as their sole magistrate, with profound silence and order, he took the gold out of the scales, and delivered it to his officers, commanding the Gauls presently to take up their scales, and to get them going. "For," sayeth he, "it is not the Romans' manner to keep their country with gold, but with the sword."

Then Brennus began to be **hot**, and told him it was not honourably done of him to break the accord that had passed between them before by oath. Whereunto Camillus stoutly answered him again, that accord was of no validity. For he had been created dictator before all other officers and magistrates whatsoever, and their acts, by his election, were made of no authority; and seeing, therefore, they had dealt with men that had no power of themselves to accord to any matter, they were to speak to him, if they **required ought**. For he alone had absolute authority to pardon them if they repented, and would ask it; or else to punish them, and make their bodies answer the damages and loss his country had by them sustained.

These words made Brennus **mad as a march hare**, that out went his blade. Then they drew their swords of all sides, and laid lustily one at another as they could, within the houses, and in open streets, where they could set no battle in order. But Brennus, suddenly remembering himself that it was no even match for him, retired with his men about him into his camp, before he had lost many of his people.

The next night following, he departed out of Rome with all his army, and went to encamp himself about sixty furlongs from thence, in the highway that goeth towards the city of the Gabians. Camillus with his whole army well appointed, went after him immediately, and appeared at his camp by the break of day. The Romans having taken heart again unto them, did lustily give them battle; it continued long, very cruel and doubtful, until the Gauls at the length were overthrown, and their camp taken with great slaughter. As for those that did escape the fury of the battle, they were killed, some by the Romans themselves, who hotly followed the chase after the battle broken: the residue of them, and the greatest part, were slain by those of the cities and villages nearabout, that did set upon them as they fled scatteringly here and there in the fields.

And thus was the city of Rome strangely again recovered, that was before strangely won and lost, after it had continued seven months in the hands of the barbarous people. For they entered Rome about the fifteenth day of July: and they were driven out again, about the thirteenth day of February following. Camillus triumphed, as he deserved, having saved his country that was lost, and brought the city, so to say, back again to itself.

For those that had fled abroad, together with their wives and children, accompanied him as he rode in; and those who had been shut up in the Capitol, and were reduced almost to the point of perishing with hunger, went out to meet him, embracing each other as they met, and weeping for joy, and, through the excess of the present pleasure, scarce believing in its truth.

The priests and ministers of the temples also, presented their holy jewels, whole and undefaced, which some of them had buried in the ground within the city itself: and others some had carried away with them, when they fled out of Rome. All these the people did as gladly see, as if the gods themselves had returned home again into their city. After they had sacrificed unto the gods, and rendered them most humble thanks, and had purified the city according to the directions of those properly instructed, he restored the existing temples, and erected a new one to ***Aius Locutius***, informing himself of the spot in which that voice came by night to Marcus Caedicius, foretelling the coming of the barbarian army. It was a matter of difficulty, and a hard task, amidst so much rubbish, to discover and re-determine the consecrated places; but by the zeal of Camillus, and the incessant labour of the priests, it was at last accomplished.

Narration and Discussion

Why did the Gauls take their final battle outside the walls of the city?

Describe ways in which Camillus showed his love for Rome.

For older students and further thought: "All these the people did as gladly see, as if the gods themselves had returned home again into their city." Why was it so important to see the jewels and religious objects restored to their places? (Compare this story with the restoration of Jerusalem in the books of Ezra and Nehemiah.)

Creative narration: This whole passage lends itself well to dramatization (possibly in Shakespearean style), newspaper reports, and other creative forms of narration.

Lesson Nine

Introduction

The rebuilding of Rome continued, though not without setbacks, and complaints (once again) that it would be easier to start afresh in the unoccupied city of Veii. However, the discovery of artifacts (such as the staff of Romulus) helped to remind the Romans of their heritage, and encouraged them to stay where they were.

Then, with "scarcely a breathing time from their trouble," they received news that an allied city was being besieged and needed help. This is one of the stories (as Plutarch explains) for which there are quite different and confusing variations. Only the first version is presented here; the second will be told in **Lesson Ten**.

Vocabulary

seditious: rebellious

tumult: upset, trouble

tarry: wait

naked and destitute: lacking even basic needs

Palatium: The Palatium was the highest point of the Palatine Hill, one of the Seven Hills of Rome; but it may mean the Palatine Hill itself.

Altar of Mars: a religious site in Rome, located in the Field of Mars

augural: used for divination (reading omens, foretelling the future)

sent to Rome: asked Rome for help

People

Romulus: the legendary founder of Rome

Historic Occasions

389 B.C.: Camillus was dictator for the third time

On the Map

Sutrium: Please read the note about historical problems in the introduction to this study.

Reading

Part One

But when they were to build again all the rest of the city, that was wholly burnt, and destroyed to the ground: the people had no mind to it, but ever shrank back to put any hand to the work, for that they lacked all things necessary to begin the same. It was a time, too, when they rather needed relief and rest from their past labours, than any new demands upon their exhausted strength and impaired fortunes. Thus they turned their thoughts again towards Veii, a city ready-built and well-provided; and gave an opening to the arts of flatterers eager to gratify their desires; and lent their ears to **seditious** language flung out against Camillus: as that, out of ambition and self-glory, he withheld them from a city fit to receive them, forcing them to live in the midst of ruins, and to re-erect a pile of burnt rubbish, that he might be esteemed not the chief magistrate only and general of Rome, but, to the exclusion of **Romulus**, its founder also.

The Senate considering of this matter, and fearing some **tumult** among the people, would not suffer Camillus to leave his dictatorship before the end of the year, though no dictator had ever held it above six months.

Then Camillus for his part did much endeavour himself to comfort and appease the people, praying them all he could to **tarry**: and further pointed with his finger unto the graves of their ancestors, and put them in mind also of the holy places dedicated to the gods, and sanctified by King Numa, or by Romulus, or by other kings *[omission for length]*.

He reminded them of the holy fire which had just been rekindled again, since the end of the war, by the vestal virgins. "What a disgrace it would be to them to lose and extinguish this, leaving the city it belonged to, to be either inhabited by strangers and newcomers, or left a wild pasture for cattle to graze on?" Such reasons as these were met, on the other hand, by laments and protestations of distress and helplessness; entreaties that, reunited, as they just were, after a sort of shipwreck, **naked and destitute**, they would not constrain them to patch up the pieces of a ruined and shattered city, when they had another at hand ready-built and prepared.

So Camillus' counsel was that the Senate should consult upon this matter, and deliver their absolute opinion herein: which was done. And in this council, he himself brought forth many probable reasons why they should not leave, in any case, the place of their natural birth and country; and so did many other senators in like case, favouring that opinion. Last of all, after these persuasions, he commanded Lucius

Lucretius (whose manner was to speak first in such assemblies) that he should stand up and deliver his opinion, and that the rest also in order as they sat, should say their minds. So every man keeping silence, as Lucretius was ready to speak, at that present time there passed by their council house a captain with his band that warded that day, who spoke aloud to his ensign bearer that went foremost, to stay, and set down his ensign there: "For," said he, "here is a very good place for us to ward in." This voice, coming in that moment of time, and at that crisis of uncertainty and anxiety for the future, was taken as a direction what was to be done; so that Lucretius, assuming an attitude of devotion, gave sentence in concurrence with the gods, as he said; and so the rest, in their order, said as much.

Moreover there was a wonderful change and alteration of mind suddenly among the common people: every one now cheered and encouraged his neighbour, and set himself to the work; proceeding in it, however, not by any regular lines or divisions, but every one pitching upon that plot of ground which came next to hand, or best pleased his fancy; by which haste and hurry in building, they constructed their city in narrow and ill-designed lanes, and with houses huddled together one upon another; for it is said that within the year the whole city was built up anew, both in its public walls and private buildings.

But the persons, however, appointed by Camillus to resume and mark out, in this general confusion, all consecrated places, coming, in their way round the **Palatium** to the **Chapel of Mars**, found the chapel itself indeed destroyed and burnt to the ground, like everything else, by the barbarians; but whilst they were clearing the place, and carrying away the rubbish, they lit upon **Romulus' augural** staff, buried under a great heap of ashes. This sort of staff is crooked at one end, and is called a *lituus*; they make use of it in quartering out the regions of the heavens when engaged in divination from the flight of birds; Romulus, who was himself a great diviner, made use of it. But when he disappeared from the earth, the priests took it, and kept it as a holy relic, suffering no creature to lay hands on it.

Now that they found this staff whole and unbroken, where all things else were consumed and perished by fire, they were in a marvellous joy thereat. For they interpreted this to be a sign of the everlasting continuance of the city of Rome.

Part Two

And now they had scarcely got a breathing time from their trouble, when a new war came upon them: the Aequians, Volscians, and Latins all at once invaded their territories, and the Tuscans besieged **Sutrium**, their confederate city. The military tribunes who commanded the army, and were encamped about Mount Marcius, being closely besieged by the Latins, and the camp in danger to be lost, **sent to Rome**, where Camillus was a third time chosen dictator.

The occasion of this war is reported two manner of ways: whereof I will declare the first, which I do conceive to be but a tale. They say the Latins sent unto the Romans, to demand some of their free maids in marriage: which they did either to make a quarrel of war, or else as desirous indeed, to join both the peoples again by new marriages. The Romans were amazed very much at this, and sore troubled, as not knowing how to answer them, they were so afraid of wars. For they were scant new settled at home, and dreaded much lest this demand of their daughters was but a summons made to give them hostages, which they finely cloaked under the name of alliance in marriage.

Some say that there was at that time a bondmaid called Tutola, or as some say, Philotis, that went unto the Senate, and counselled them they should send her away with some other fair maids' slaves, dressed up like gentlewomen, and then let her alone. The Senate liked very well of this device, and chose such a number of bondmaids as she desired to have, and trimming them up in fine apparel, begauded with chains of gold and jewels, they sent them forth to the Latins, who were encamped not far from the city.

When night was come, the other maids hid their enemies' swords. But this Tutola, or Philotis (call her as you will) did climb up to the top of a wild fig tree, from which she shewed a burning torch unto the Romans, and spreading out a woolen cloth behind her, held out a torch towards Rome, which was the signal between her and the commanders, without the knowledge, however, of any other of the citizens, which was the reasons that their issuing out from the city was tumultuous, the officers pushing their men on, and they calling one another's names, and scarce able to bring themselves into order; that setting upon the enemy's works, who either were asleep or expected no such matter, they took the camp and destroyed most of them.

[Omission for length]

Narration and Discussion

What difficulties did Camillus face in rebuilding Rome? How did he overcome them?

Why did Plutarch consider the story of the disguised slave girls to be probably just a fable? Do you think it could have happened?

Lesson Ten

Introduction

Camillus, at the age of about sixty, was still a top military strategist, and quite capable of leading the Roman forces against enemy tribes. Even those who had previously called him "just lucky" were forced to admit that skill and courage might also have contributed to his success.

Vocabulary

palisade: wall constructed of stakes, for defense

fiery matter: Dryden, "combustibles"; things set on fire

commiserating their case: full of sympathy for them

conjecturing: guessing

Historic Occasions

389 B.C.: Camillus conquered rival nations and had his third triumph

On the Map

the mountain Maecius: in Latin, *ad Maecium*

Sutrium: possibly Satricum; see introductory note

Reading

Part One

The other account of the war (according to the general stream of writers) is this: Camillus, being the third time chosen dictator, and learning that the army under the tribunes was besieged by the Latins and Volscians, was constrained to arm not only those under, but also those over, the age of service; and taking a large circuit round **the mountain Maecius**, undiscovered by the enemy, lodged his army behind them, where he raised fires to make the Romans that were besieged know how he was come. The besieged, encouraged by this, prepared to sally forth and join battle; but the Latins and Volscians, fearing this exposure to an enemy on both sides, drew themselves within their works, and fortified their camp with a strong **palisade** of trees on every side, resolving to wait for more supplies from home, and expecting also the assistance of the Tuscans, their confederates.

Camillus perceiving this, and fearing lest they should serve him, as he had already handled them, by compassing of him again behind: he thought it necessary to prevent this. So considering the enclosure and fortification of their camp was all of wood, and that every morning, commonly, there came a great wind from the side of the mountains, he provided a number of torches. And leading out his army into the fields by break of day, he appointed one part of them to give charge upon the enemies on the one side, with great noise and shouting: and he with the other part determined to raise fire on the contrary side, from whence the wind should come, looking for opportunity to do the same. When he saw the sun up, and the wind beginning to whistle, blowing a good gale from the side of the hills, and that the skirmish was begun on the other side: then he gave a signal of onset; and heaving in an infinite quantity of **fiery matter**, filled all their rampart with it, so that the flame being fed by the close timber and wooden palisades, went on and spread into all quarters. The Latins, having nothing ready to keep it off or extinguish it, when the camp was now almost full of fire, were driven back within a very small compass, and at last forced by necessity to come into their enemy's hands, who stood before the works ready armed and prepared to receive them; of these very few escaped, while those that stayed in the camp were all a prey to the fire, until the Romans themselves came to quench it, for greediness of their spoil and goods.

Part Two

When all this was done, Camillus left his son in the camp, to keep the prisoners and spoils; and he himself, with the rest of the army, went to invade his enemies' country, where he took Bola, the capital city of the Aequians.

Then after he had overcome the Volsces, he led his army to **Sutrium**: not having heard what had befallen the Sutrians, but making haste to assist them, as if they were still in danger and besieged by the Tuscans. They, however, had already surrendered their city to their enemies; and destitute of all things, with nothing left but their clothes, met Camillus on the way, lamenting their misery, with their wives and little young children: whose misery went to the very heart of Camillus, when he beheld their lamentable state. Furthermore, when he saw the soldiers weeping, and **commiserating their case**, while the Sutrians hung about and clung to them, resolved not to defer revenge, but that very day to lead his army to Sutrium; **conjecturing** that the enemy, having just taken a rich and plentiful city, without an enemy left within it, nor any from without to be expected, would be found abandoned to enjoyment, and unguarded.

And indeed it fell out rightly as he guessed. For he had not only passed through the territories of the city, without any intelligence given to the enemies within the same: but he was come to the very gates, and had taken the walls, before they heard anything of his coming, by reason they neither kept watch nor ward, but were dispersed abroad in the city, in every house, eating and drinking drunk together. Insomuch as when they knew their enemies were already within the city, they were so full with meat and wine, that the most of their wits served them not so much as to flee, but tarried until they were slain or taken like beasts in the houses.

Thus was the city of Sutrium twice taken in one day. And it chanced that those which had won it, lost it; and those which had lost it, recovered it again by Camillus' means. For all which actions he received a triumph, which brought him no less honour and reputation than the two former ones; for those citizens who before most regarded him with an evil eye, and ascribed his successes to a certain luck rather than real merit, were compelled by these last acts of his to confess that his wisdom and valiantness deserved praise and commendation to the skies.

Narration and Discussion

Choose three adjectives that you think best describe Camillus at this point in his life.

Creative narration: You are a Roman reporter on the day of Camillus' third triumph. Chat with anyone you can find who might have an opinion about whether he deserved this honour. If you can manage an exclusive interview with Camillus himself, so much the better.

Lesson Eleven

Introduction

Well into old age, Camillus continued to be a powerful force in Rome. He outwitted a political rebel who had been playing on people's memories of his past glories; and led troops in battle (though somewhat reluctantly). His one blind (or at least overly generous) spot seemed to be the Tusculans.

Vocabulary

usurpation: taking, seizing

gain the multitude: get the support of the common people

changed their apparel: put on mourning clothes

manifest: unarguable, obvious

Moneta: a version of the goddess Juno

being called again to his sixth tribuneship: This was in reaction to a new military crisis involving Antium and other Volsci cities, which had united and retaken Sutrium (or Satricum, see notes).

ensue upon: follow

one of his companions: Other sources state that Lucius Furius was the son or nephew of Camillus.

protract the war: To protract something is to prolong or extend it; but here it seems that Camillus wanted to delay the battle.

stayed: ceased, stopped

exceeding spoil: large amount of treasure

made suit to have the charge: wanted to be in office

fetches: tricks

the privilege and freedom of Rome: the rights of citizens

People

Marcus Manlius: see **Lesson Seven**

Quinctius Capitolinus: Titus Quinctius Cincinnatus Capitolinus, dictator in 380 B.C. (Plutarch says that he was dictator during the Marcus Manlius events, but other sources say that he was Master of the Horse, second to Aulus Cornelius Cossus.)

Historic Occasions

384 B.C.: Camillus was consular tribune (fifth time)

384 B.C.: Execution of Marcus Manlius

381 B.C.: Camillus was consular tribune (sixth and last time)

On the Map

Tusculum (Tusculans): Not to be confused with the Tuscans of

Tuscany! Tusculum was a city southeast of Rome, the original home of the Furii (Camillus' family).

Reading

Part One

Camillus, of all his enemies, had one most bitter to him, which was **Marcus Manlius**, that was the first man that gave the Gauls the repulse that night they had entered the walls of the Capitol, and had thought to have taken it; and who for that reason had been named Capitolinus. He, aspiring to be the chief of the city, and finding no direct way to exceed the glory of Camillus, took that ordinary course towards **usurpation** of absolute power, namely, to **gain the multitude**, those of them especially that were in debt; defending some by pleading their causes against their creditors; rescuing others by force, and not suffering the law to proceed against them; insomuch that in a short time he got great numbers of indigent people about him, whose tumults and uproars in the Forum struck terror into the principal citizens.

After **Quinctius Capitolinus**, who was made dictator to suppress these disorders, had committed Manlius to prison, the people immediately **changed their apparel**, a thing never done but in great and public calamities; and the Senate, fearing some tumult, ordered him to be released. He being thus out of prison, was no whit the better, nor wiser thereby, but did still stir up the commons, more boldly and seditiously, than before.

They chose, therefore, Camillus (for the fifth time) as military tribune; and a day being appointed for Manlius to answer to his charge, the view from the place where his trial was held proved a great impediment to his accusers; for the very spot where Manlius by night fought with the Gauls overlooked the Forum from the Capitol, so that, he himself pointing with his hand, showed the place unto the gods, and weeping tenderly, he laid before them the remembrance of the hazard of his life, in fighting for their safety. This did move the judges' hearts to pity, so as they knew not what to do; but many times they did put over the hearing of his case unto another day, and neither would they give judgement, knowing he was convicted by **manifest** proofs:

neither could they use the severity of the law upon him, because the place of his so notable good service was ever still before their eyes.

Wherefore Camillus, finding the cause of delay of justice, did make the place of judgement to be removed without the city, into a place called the Peteline Grove, from whence they could not see the Capitol. And there the accusers gave apparent evidence against him: and the judges considering all his wicked practices, conceived a just cause to punish him, as he had deserved. He was convicted, carried to the Capitol, and flung headlong from the rock; so that one and the same spot was thus the witness of his greatest glory, and monument of his most unfortunate end.

The Romans, besides, razed his house, and built there a temple to the goddess they call **Moneta**, ordaining for the future that none of the patrician order should ever dwell on the Capitoline.

Part Two

Camillus after this, **being called again to his sixth tribuneship**, desired to be excused, as being aged, and perhaps not unfearful of the malice of Fortune, and those reverses which seem to **ensue upon** great prosperity.

Howbeit the most apparent cause of his excuse, was his sickness, which troubled him much at that time. But the people would allow no excuse by any means, but cried out they did not desire he should fight afoot, nor a-horseback, but that he should only give counsel and command; and, therefore, they compelled him to take the charge, and to lead the army with **one of his companions**, named Lucius Furius, against the enemy. These were the Praenestines, and the Volsces, who, with large forces, were laying waste the territory of the Roman confederates.

Having marched out with his army, he sat down and encamped near the enemy, meaning himself to **protract the war**, or, if there should come any necessity or occasion of fighting, in the meantime to regain his strength. But Lucius Furius, contrarily coveting glory, was hotly bent to hazard the battle, whatsoever peril came of it: and to this end he stirred up and encouraged the captains of every private band. Wherefore Camillus fearing he might be seen out of envy to be wishing to rob the young men of the glory of a noble exploit, consented, though unwillingly, that he (Lucius Furius) should draw out the forces, whilst himself, by reason of weakness, stayed behind with a few in the camp.

Lucius went on ahead to present battle to the enemy, but was quickly overthrown. But Camillus, hearing the Romans were overthrown, could not contain himself; but, leaping from his bed, with those he had about him ran to meet them at the gates of the camp, passing through those that fled, until he came to meet with the enemies that had them in chase. The Romans seeing this that were already entered into the camp, followed him at the heels: and those that fled also without, when they saw him, they gathered together, and put themselves again in array before him, and persuaded one another not to forsake their captain. So their enemies hereupon **stayed** their chasing, and would pursue no further that day.

But the next morning, Camillus leading his army into the field, gave them battle, and won the field of them by plain force: and following the victory hard, he entered amongst them that fled into their camp pell-mell, and slew the most part of them even there.

After this victory, he was advertised how the Tuscans had taken the city of Sutrium, and had put to the sword all the inhabitants of the same, who were Roman citizens. Whereupon he sent to Rome the greatest part of his army, and keeping with him the lightest and lustiest men, went and gave assault unto the Tuscans, that now were harboured in the city of Sutrium. Which when he had won again, he slew part of them; and the others saved themselves by flight.

Part Three

After this, he returned to Rome with an **exceeding spoil**, confirming by experience the wisdom of the Romans, who did not fear the age nor sickness of a good captain that was expert and valiant; but had chosen him against his will, though he was both old and sick, and preferred him far before the younger and lustier that **made suit to have the charge**.

When, therefore, the revolt of the **Tusculans** was reported, they gave Camillus the charge of reducing them, choosing one of his five colleagues to go with him. And when everyone was eager for the place, contrary to the expectation of all, he passed by the rest and chose

Lucius Furius, the very same man who lately, against the judgement of Camillus, had rashly hazarded and nearly lost a battle. Howbeit Camillus, having a desire (as I think) to hide his fault and shame he had received, did of courtesy prefer him before all others.

Now the Tusculans, hearing of Camillus' coming against them, made a cunning attempt at revoking their act of revolt; their fields, as in times of highest peace, were full of ploughmen and shepherds; their gates stood wide open, and their children were being taught in the schools; of the people, such as were tradesmen, he found in their workshops, busied about their various employments; and the better sort of citizens walking in the public places in their ordinary dress; the magistrates hurried about to provide quarters for the Romans, as if they stood in fear of no danger and were conscious of no fault.

Howbeit all these fine **fetches** could not make Camillus believe but that they had an intent to rebel against the Romans; yet they made Camillus pity them, seeing they repented them of that which they had determined to do. So he commanded them to go to Rome to the Senate, to crave pardon of their fault; and he himself did help them not only to purge their city of any intent of rebellion, but also to get them **the privilege and freedom of Rome**. And these be the chiefest acts Camillus did in the sixth time of his tribuneship.

Narration and Discussion

Why was Camillus reluctant to take the office of tribune again? Should he have refused?

Tell the story of Lucius Furius. Was it good judgement on Camillus' part to give him another chance?

For further thought: It has been suggested that Camillus may have had a soft spot for the Tusculans, since they were (in a way) his own people. What do you think?

Creative narration: Imagine that you are one of Camillus' trusted friends. Write or act out an imagined conversation after these events. What would you advise him to do next? Is it time for him to retire?

Lesson Twelve and Examination Questions

Introduction

A common pattern in Plutarch's *Lives* is for things to go along quite well until near the end; and then his subject makes one big mistake and is punished, or an enemy assassinates him. However, that doesn't happen in this story. Camillus did come close to being arrested during the patrician-plebeian consul crisis, but he stood his ground, and was given some of the credit for its resolution.

Vocabulary

general muster: a military registration. Camillus was trying to keep the plebeian council from meeting (and approving the demand that one of the consuls be a plebeian).

general of horse: second-in-command, lieutenant

appease the dissension: calm the hostility

baser: lower class

sitting upon the tribunal: acting as judge

Concord: Concordia was the Roman goddess of peace and harmony.

one should be chosen from the commonalty: The new office of **praetor** (see introductory notes) was also created at this time, and was open to both classes.

People

Licinius Stolo: Gaius Licinius Calvus Stolo, tribune from 376 to 367 B.C.

Marcus Aemilius: or Lucius Aemilius Mamercinus; consul in 366 and 363 B.C.

Lucius Sextius: Lucius Sextius Lateranus, consul in 366 B.C.

Historic Occasions

376 B.C.: Bill proposed that one consul must be of the plebeian class

368 B.C.: Camillus chosen dictator for the fourth time

367 B.C.: Camillus chosen dictator for the fifth time, to oppose the Gauls

367 B.C.: The building of the Temple of Concord

366 B.C.: The first plebeian consul elected

365 B.C.: Death of Camillus

Reading

Part One

After these things, **Licinius Stolo** moved great sedition in the city between the common people and the Senate. For he would in any case that of the two consuls, which were chosen yearly, one of them should be a commoner, and not that both of them should be of the ancient noble families, called Patricians. Tribunes of the people were chosen, but the election of the consuls was interrupted and prevented by the people. And as this absence of any supreme magistrate was leading to yet further confusion, Camillus was the fourth time created dictator by the Senate, sorely against the people's will, and not altogether in accordance with his own; he had little desire for a conflict with men whose past services entitled them to tell him that he had achieved far greater actions in war along with them than in politics with the patricians, who, indeed, had only put him forward now out of envy; that, if successful, he might crush the people, or failing, be crushed himself.

However, to provide as good a remedy as he could for the present, knowing the day on which the tribunes of the people intended to propose the law, he appointed that day, by proclamation, for a **general**

muster, and called the people from the Forum into the Field of Mars, threatening to set heavy fines upon such as should not obey.

On the other side, the tribunes of the people met his threats by solemnly protesting they would fine him in fifty thousand drachmas of silver, if he persisted in obstructing the people from giving their voices to such law as they liked of. Camillus perceiving this, and fearing to be condemned, and banished once again, which would fall out very ill for him, being now an old man, and one that had done so many great and notable acts, or else for that he thought himself not strong enough to withstand the force of the people: he kept his house that day, feigning himself to be sick, and certain other days following; and in the end he gave up his office.

The Senate created another dictator, who, choosing Stolo, leader of the sedition, to be his **general of horse**, suffered that law to be passed by voices of the people, that above all other laws, which was most grievous to the patricians, namely, that no person whatsoever should possess above five hundred acres of land. Stolo was much distinguished by the victory he had gained; but, not long after, was found himself to possess more than he had allowed to others, and suffered the penalties of his own law.

Part Two

And now the contention about election of consuls coming on (which was the main point and original cause of the dissension, and had throughout furnished most matter of division between the Senate and the people), certain intelligence arrived that the Gauls again, proceeding from the Adriatic Sea, were marching in vast numbers upon Rome. On the very heels of the report followed manifest acts also of hostility; the country through which they marched was all wasted, and such as by flight could not make their escape to Rome were dispersing and scattering among the mountains.

The fear of this did somewhat **appease the dissension**. The people then assembling with the Senate, and the **baser** sort with the noble, did all with one voice and assent chose Camillus as dictator the fifth time.

[Omission for length: Camillus, though close to eighty years old, distinguished

himself once again in battle against the Gauls; Vellitri also surrendered to Rome; and Camillus was given a final triumph.]

Part Three

But the greatest of all civil contests, and the hardest to be managed, was still to be fought out against the common people, who, returning home full of victory and success, insisted, contrary to established law, to have one of the consuls chosen out of their own body.

The Senate strongly opposed it, and would not suffer Camillus to lay down his dictatorship, thinking that, under the shelter of his great name and authority, they should be better able to contend for the power of his aristocracy. But when Camillus was **sitting upon the tribunal**, despatching public affairs, an officer, sent by the tribunes of the people, commanded him to rise and follow him, laying his hand upon him, as ready to seize and carry him away; upon which, such a noise and tumult as was never heard before filled the whole Forum: some that were about Camillus thrusting the officer from the bench, and the multitude below calling out to him to bring Camillus down.

This so amazed Camillus, that he knew not well what to say to the matter. Notwithstanding, he would not resign up his office, but taking those senators he had about him, he went unto the place where the Senate was wont to be kept. And there, before he would go into it, he returned back again unto the Capitol, and made his prayer unto the gods, that it would please them to bring his troubles again to a quiet, and so made a solemn vow and promise (if these tumults and troubles might be pacified) that he would build a temple to **Concord**.

A great conflict of opposite opinions arose in the Senate; but, at last, the most moderate and most acceptable to the people prevailed, and consent was given, that, of two consuls, **one should be chosen from the commonalty**.

When the dictator proclaimed this determination of the Senate to the people, at the moment pleased and reconciled with the Senate, as indeed could not otherwise be, they accompanied Camillus home, with all expressions and acclamations of joy; and the next day, assembling together, they voted a temple of Concord to be built, according to Camillus' vow, facing the assembly and the Forum; and to the feasts, called the Latin Holidays, they added one more, making four in all, and ordained that, on the present occasion, the whole people of Rome should sacrifice with garlands on their heads.

In the election of consuls held by Camillus, **Marcus Aemilius** was chosen of the patricians, and **Lucius Sextius** the first of the commonalty; and this was the last of all Camillus' actions.

For, the next year after, the plague was in Rome, and took away an infinite number of people that died, besides many magistrates and officers of the city that departed: among whom, Camillus also left his life. Who notwithstanding he had lived a long time, and had ended a reasonable course of life: yet he was as ready to die, and as patiently took his death, as any man living could have done. Moreover, the Romans made more moan and lamentation for his death alone, than for all the rest the plague had already consumed.

Narration and Discussion

When the civil unrest was ended, Camillus built a temple to Concord. How would you mark the end of a quarrel or an unhappy time? (Look up 1 Samuel 7:12 for a Biblical example.)

Why did the Romans make such "moan and lamentation" for the death of Camillus?

Creative narration #1: You are the Roman schoolteacher from **Lesson One**, trying to explain the government reforms to your class of young students. What questions might they have?

Creative narration #2: If Shakespeare had written a play called *Camillus*, how might it have ended?

Examination Questions

Younger Students:

1. Tell how the Romans retook their city from the Gauls.

2. Why did Camillus never become a consul of Rome?

Older Students:

1. What difficulties did Camillus face in rebuilding Rome? How did he overcome them? OR Answer Question 2.

2. (High school) Tell the story of Camillus' impeachment and exile. Was it justified?

Dion of Syracuse

(408-354 B.C.)

Who was Dion?

This story is set in the mid-fourth century B.C., in the city-state of Syracuse on the island of Sicily. It's the story of two father-and-son tyrant rulers who called themselves kings, both named Dionysius. But the main character is Dion (pronounced Dion as in Lion), who was a relative, mentor, and finally mortal enemy to the second Dionysius. It has been pointed out that Dion and his siblings, as the children of Hipparinus, a wealthy and powerful man, had a social status that the upstart Dionysius I lacked, which suggests that envy might have been partially to blame for the increasing conflict between the families. However, Dionysius was clever enough to make use of Dion's connections in his dealings with other rulers, where he himself, perhaps, might not have been shown as much respect.

What was Syracuse?

The city-state of Syracuse was located in the southeastern corner of the island of Sicily. We now associate Sicily with Italy rather than

Greece, but Syracuse was a Greek city, founded by the city of Corinth and also allied with Sparta. It was divided into "quarters," or neighbourhoods, including Acradina, Ortygia (also spelled Ortigia), and Epipoli (Epipolae).

Trivia Question #1: *What famous mathematician and engineer was born in Syracuse? (Answers to trivia questions are below.)*

What is a tyrant?

The idea of a "tyrant king" in Ancient Greece was somewhat different from the way we use the word "tyrant" today. It meant an absolute ruler and it wasn't a judgment about whether he was good or evil. (Compare this with the Roman idea of a dictator from the same era, as in the *Life of Camillus*.)

However, the tyranny of Dionysius I and his son caused resentment in Syracuse, because he was a military hero who had been elected to a top government position but had then taken full control and, essentially, made himself king. Plutarch calls both father and son "the tyrant" or "the **Usurper**," meaning one who takes power illegally or by force. He almost never refers to either of them as king.

Dion himself is also referred to as "Tyrant of Syracuse," although he held that position for only a short time.

Trivia Question #2: *What person in the Bible stayed at Syracuse?*

What was Carthage?

In Mary Renault's novel about Dion (see the note that follows), a visitor to Syracuse was surprised at the numerous fortifications that Dionysius had put in place. Someone else explained, "Nothing here makes sense, without the Carthaginians."

Carthage, like Syracuse, was both a city and a state, located just across the sea from Sicily, in present-day Tunisia. By the era of Dionysius I and Dion, it was a major power in the western Mediterranean. The Syracusans' fear of the Carthaginians was, apparently, what kept them from rebelling against the tyrant Dionysius, and also what motivated them to pay high taxes and spend their own time working to build the walls and war machinery.

Trivia Question #3: *What saint, whose feast day is December 13, was born in Syracuse?*

What was the castle?

Ortygia, an island just across from the rest of the city, was a natural fortress, and had been the original site of Syracuse. (Mary Renault called it "not a fort, but a hidden city.")

Another "castle" was the **Euryalus Fortress**, which was built on a hill called **Epipolae**, to protect Syracuse from Carthaginian attack.

It would seem that most of the military events in the story, such as the siege, took place around Ortygia. However, there are references to the Epipolae as well, and as it was also close to the sea, it is not impossible that, for example, Dion's abduction took place there rather than at Ortygia.

Some students may wonder how the Syracusans accessed an island fortress: did they need boats? The answer is that in about 550 B.C., the colonists built a causeway, or raised road, to the island.

The role of Greek philosophy in this story

As described in **Lesson One**, Dion's heart was "set aflame" when he began to study philosophy with Plato. Among other things, Plato emphasized the need for **virtue** in one's life. Virtue was defined as moral excellence, but it also included valour (bravery) and physical strength. He named four cardinal, or key, virtues: prudence, fortitude, temperance (moderation and self-control), and justice.

Another point about philosophy is that, in the ancient world, it was not limited to topics such as beauty and evil, but covered many kinds of knowledge, including astronomy, medicine, and physics.

> ***"It's all in Plato, all in Plato: bless me, what do they teach them at these schools?" (C.S. Lewis, The Last Battle)***

A note about historical fiction

Adults and older high school students may be interested in reading *The*

Mask of Apollo, by Mary Renault (Cox & Wyman Ltd., 1966), from which I have drawn one or two points. However, it is not recommended for younger readers because of its adult themes.

Answer to trivia questions: Archimedes; Paul (Acts 28:12); St. Lucy (Santa Lucia).

Top Vocabulary Terms in the Life of Dion

If you know these words, you're well on the way to mastering the vocabulary for this study. They will not be repeated in the lessons.

1. **divers:** different, separate; several

2. **familiars:** close friends

3. **fetch:** trick

4. **galley:** a ship powered both by sails and by banks of oars

5. **hard by:** near to

6. **mercenary:** Mercenary soldiers are those hired to fight for pay, who do not have a personal interest in the outcome. **"Soldiers who were strangers"** also refers to mercenaries.

7. **mutiny:** to rebel against one's leader

8. **practice, practise:** plan, plot, scheme. British/Canadian spelling differentiates between the noun and the verb; Americans use **practice** for both. However, the word is also used with its more common meaning: for instance, in **Lesson Nine**, the sailors were "men practised to fight by sea."

9. **strait:** tight, narrow. To do things straitly means to use strictness, not allowing any leeway. To be in "dire straits" is to be in a dangerous situation. A strait is also a waterway, such as the Strait of Messina between Sicily and mainland Italy.

10. **tarry:** wait

 Bonus term: Victuals (pronounced "vittles") are food supplies, also called **provisions**.

Lesson One

Introduction

Brought up under the rule of a tyrant "king" (see the introductory notes for this study), Dion might have been headed for a life of bitterness and unhappiness. However, Dion became a valued member of the royal court, first because his sister was married to the king, but also on his own merits. Along the way, he ran into the philosopher Plato, who happened to be visiting Sicily. Plutarch says that, on being introduced to the philosophy of virtue over material success, his heart was immediately "set aflame."

Vocabulary

established himself in his government: a nice way of saying that Dionysius had seized power in Syracuse

to compensate her…: to make up for her not being Syracusan

issue: children

an honourable reception: a welcome at the royal court

worth and parts: character and abilities (see the introductory notes)

virtue: see introductory notes

servility: wanting excessively to please others. In this context it may refer to the "servile" people surrounding the tyrant.

intimidation: rule by threat of punishment

obtained the favour of him…: got Dionysius to agree, when he had some free time

fortitude: bravery, courage

valiant: brave, showing valour

lost your labour: wasted your time

alluding to his name: Gelon means "to laugh"

quibble: joke

People

Dionysius I or "The Elder": see introductory notes

Doris and **Aristomache:** the two wives of Dionysius I

Gelon: the founder of Syracuse, known for his generous nature

Historic Occasions

432 B.C.: Birth of Dionysius I

428/427 or 424/423 B.C.: Birth of Plato

409 B.C.: War against **Carthage** (see introductory notes), in which Dionysius I distinguished himself as a military leader

408 B.C.: Birth of Dion

406 B.C.: Dionysius I elected to a high government position in Syracuse

405 B.C.: Dionysius I seized full control of Syracuse

402-397 B.C.: Construction of the Euryalus Castle

c. 397 B.C.: Birth of Dionysius II

397-392 B.C. Further wars with Carthage; it is likely that Dion began his military career towards the end of this time

387 B.C.: Possible date of Plato's first visit to Syracuse

On the Map

On a map (preferably one showing this era), locate the Mediterranean Sea, the Ionian Sea, Italy, Sicily, Syracuse, Carthage, Greece, Corinth, and Sparta (Lacedaemon).

Aegina (Aeginetes): a Greek island near Athens

Reading

Part One

[Some introductory paragraphs are omitted for length.]

Dionysius the Elder first married the daughter of Hermocrates, a citizen of Syracuse.

[omission for content: his first wife died under sad circumstances]

But after he had **established himself in his government**, he married again two other wives together: the one a stranger of the city of Locres, called **Doris**; and the other a native of Sicily, called **Aristomache**, the daughter of Hipparinus, the chiefest man of all Syracuse, who had been companion with Dionysius the first time he was chosen general. It was said that Dionysius married them both in one day, and that he made as much of the one as he did of the other; though the Syracusans would have their own countrywoman preferred before the stranger. Howbeit Doris, **to compensate her for her foreign extraction**, had the good fortune to be the mother of the son and heir of the family; while Aristomache continued for a long time without **issue**, though Dionysius was very desirous to have children by her: so much so that he put her own mother to death, accusing her that she had with sorceries and witchcraft kept Aristomache from being with child.

Dion, Aristomache's brother, at first found **an honourable reception** for his sister's sake; but his own **worth and parts** soon procured him a nearer place in his brother-in-law's affection, who, among other favours, gave special command to his treasurers to furnish Dion with whatever money he demanded, only telling him on the same day what they had delivered out.

Now though Dion was before reputed a person of lofty character, of a noble mind, and daring courage, yet these excellent qualifications all received a great development when Plato by good fortune arrived in Sicily, and became acquainted with Dion. Dion was but a young man at that time, but yet had an apter wit to learn, and readier goodwill to follow **virtue**, than any young man else that followed Plato: as Plato himself writeth, and his own doings also do witness.

For Dion having from a child been brought up with humble conditions under a tyrant, accustomed to a life on the one hand of **servility** and **intimidation**, and yet on the other of vulgar display and luxury, the mistaken happiness of people that knew no better thing than pleasure and self-indulgence, yet, at the first taste of reason and a philosophy that demands obedience to virtue, his soul was set aflame; and in the simple innocence of youth, concluding, from his own disposition, that the same reason would work the same effects upon Dionysius, he made it his business, and at length **obtained the favour of him, at a leisure hour**, to hear Plato.

Part Two

When Plato came to Dionysius, all their talk in manner was of virtue, and they chiefly reasoned what "**fortitude**" was: wherein Plato proved that tyrants were no **valiant** men. From thence, passing further into "justice," he asserted the happy estate of the just, and the miserable condition of the unjust. These arguments Dionysius would not hear out; but, feeling himself, as it were, convicted by Plato's words, and much displeased to see the rest of the bystanders full of admiration for the speaker and having such delight to hear him speak, at last, exceedingly exasperated, he asked the philosopher in a rage what business he had in Sicily. To which Plato answered, "I came to seek a virtuous man."

"It seems then," replied Dionysius, "you have **lost your labour**."

Now Dion thought that Dionysius' anger would proceed no further, and therefore at Plato's earnest request, he sent him away in a galley with three banks of oars, which was conveying Pollis, a Lacedaemonian captain, back into Greece. Howbeit, Dionysius secretly requested Pollis to kill Plato by the way, as ever he would do him pleasure: if not, yet that he would sell him for a slave, howsoever he did. "For," said he, "he shall be nothing the worse for that: because if he be a just man, he shall be as happy to be a slave, as a free man." Thus, as it is reported, this Pollis carried Plato into the isle of **Aegina**, and there sold him. For the Aeginetes, having war at that time with the Athenians, made a decree that all the Athenians that were taken in their isle should be sold.

Part Three

This notwithstanding, Dion was not in less favour and credit with Dionysius than formerly; but was entrusted with matters of great weight, and sent on important embassies to Carthage, in the management of which he gained very great reputation. Besides, the Usurper (Dionysius) bore with the liberty he (Dion) took to speak his mind freely, he being the only man who, upon any occasion, dared boldly say what he thought: as, for example, in the rebuke he gave him (Dionysius) about **Gelon**. Dionysius was ridiculing Gelon's government, and, **alluding to his name**, said he had been the laughing stock of Sicily. While others seemed to admire and applaud the **quibble**, Dion very warmly replied, "Nevertheless, it is certain that you are sole governor here because you were trusted for Gelon's sake; but for your sake no man will ever hereafter be trusted again." For, indeed, Gelon had made a monarchy appear the best, whereas Dionysius had convinced men that it was the worst of governments.

Narration and Discussion

Tell what you know about Dion's early life.

Why do you think the relationship between Plato and Dionysius didn't work out well?

What does it say about Dion's character and reputation that Dionysius still respected and trusted him after the Plato incident?

For further thought: We often grow up assuming that our own experience is the "norm"; but then something or someone causes us to view it with new eyes. How might this have been true of Dion?

Creative narration: Choose a scene from this passage, such as the Dion trying to convince Dionysius to arrange a meeting with Plato, or the "philosophy lesson"; and either expand it in writing or act it out.

Lesson Two

Introduction

In the first reading, we met Dionysius I, the tyrant ruler of Syracuse. When he died, he left his son Dionysius II as his successor; but, as the younger Dionysius had no training in matters of state, and had been brought up only to please himself, Syracuse became even more unsettled than it had been under his father.

Dion continued to apply his philosophical principles to his influential position as an advisor to the new king. His extremely serious attitude, however, did not please everyone.

Vocabulary

Dion married her, being his niece: Dion's sister was married to the king, so Dionysius I was his brother-in-law; but he later married his niece Arete, the daughter of that same sister and the king, making Dionysius I also his father-in-law, and Dionysius II his brother-in-law (doubly so because Dionysius II married the sister of Arete).

ingratiate themselves: put themselves in favour

insensibility: state of unconsciousness

followed by his death: Plutarch implies that he was given an overdose of medicine; other accounts say that a play he wrote won a prize and that he became ill after too much celebration. Possibly both are true.

advance his interest: make him successful

evil brought-up: the unfortunate early training of Dionysius II will be described in **Lesson Three**

drunken debauch: wild party

many days: translations vary in the number of days given

buffoonery: crazy behaviour

construed into reprimand: taken as criticism

censured: scolded, criticized

misdemeanours: sins, crimes

fine: sensitive

austere: plain to the point of being harsh

obstinacy: stubbornness, refusal to move

in tickle state: a situation that might turn disastrous if not handled carefully

People

Arete: daughter of Aristomache. Dion, her uncle, became her second husband.

Historic Occasions

367 B.C.: Death of Dionysius I

Reading

Part One

Dionysius the Elder had by his Locrian wife, Doris, three children; and by Aristomache four, of the which two were daughters, the one called Sophrosyne, and the other **Arete**. Of them, Dionysius' eldest son married Sophrosyne, and Arete was married unto his brother Thearides, after whose death **Dion married her, being his niece**.

Now, when Dionysius was sick and likely to die, Dion endeavoured to speak with him on behalf of the children he (Dionysius) had by

Aristomache; but he was prevented by the physicians, who wanted to **ingratiate themselves** with the next successor; who also, as Timaeus reports, gave him a sleeping potion which he asked for, which produced an **insensibility** only **followed by his death**.

Part Two

Nevertheless, at the first council which the young Dionysius held with his friends, Dion discoursed so well of the present state of affairs that he made all the rest appear in their politics but children, and in their votes rather slaves than counsellors, who, in a beastly and cowardly manner, advised what would please the young man, rather than what would **advance his interest**. But that which startled them most was the proposal he made to avert the imminent danger they feared of a war with the Carthaginians, undertaking, if Dionysius wanted peace, to sail immediately over into Africa, and conclude it there upon honourable terms; but, if he rather preferred war, then he would fit out and maintain, at his own cost and charges, fifty galleys ready to row.

Dionysius wondered much at his greatness of mind, and received his offer with satisfaction. But the other courtiers, thinking his generosity reflected upon them, and jealous of being lessened by his greatness, from hence took all occasions to accuse him, not sparing any reproachful words against him, to move Dionysius to be offended with him. For they complained of him, and said that he cunningly practised to possess the tyranny, making himself strong by sea, going about by his galleys to make the tyranny fall into the hands of the children of Aristomache his sister.

But the chiefest cause of all why they did malice and hate him was his strange manner of life: that he neither would keep company with them, nor live after their manner. For they that from the beginning were crept in favour and friendship with this young **evil-brought-up** tyrant (Dionysius II), by flattering of him, and feeding him with vain pleasures, studied for no other thing but to entertain him in love matters and other vain exercises, such as to riot and banquet, and all such other vile vicious pastimes and recreations *[omission for length and content]*. It is reported of him that, having begun a **drunken debauch**, he continued it **many days** without intermission; in all which time no person on business was allowed to appear, nor was any serious conversation heard at court, but drinking, singing, dancing, and **buffoonery** reigned there without control.

It is likely then they had little kindness for Dion, who never indulged himself in any youthful pleasure or diversion: whereupon they accused him, and misnamed his virtues vices, being somewhat to be resembled unto them. They called his gravity, "pride"; his plainness and boldness in his oration, "obstinacy"; the good advice he gave was all **construed into reprimand**; and he was **censured** for neglecting and scorning those in whose **misdemeanours** he declined to participate. For to say truly, his manners by nature had a certain haughtiness of mind and severity, and he was a sour man to be acquainted with: whereby his company was not only troublesome, but also unpleasant to this younger Dionysius, whose ears were so **fine** that they could not stand to hear anything but flattery.

And furthermore, divers of his very friends and familiars, that did like and commend his plain manner of speech and noble mind, they did yet reprove his sternness, and **austere** conversation with men. For it seemed unto them that he spoke too roughly and dealt overhardly with them that had to do with him, and more than became a civil or courteous man. And for proof hereof, Plato himself sometime wrote unto him (as if he had prophesied what should happen) that he should beware of **obstinacy**, the companion of solitariness, that bringeth a man in the end to be forsaken of everyone.

This notwithstanding, they did more reverence him at that time than any man else, because of the state and government, and for that they thought him the only man that could best provide for the safety and quietness of the tyranny, the which stood then **in tickle state**.

Narration and Discussion

Dion criticized the men of the assembly because they, "in a beastly and cowardly manner, advised what would please the young man, rather than what would advance his interest." Why would that make them beastly and cowardly? What kind of counsel and advice did Dion prefer to give? Which way shows more true loyalty? (See Prov. 24:24-25)

Creative narration: Write a conversation between two Syracusans, one who thinks Dion is a valuable asset to the government and a good person to have around, and another who wishes they could rid themselves of him.

For further thought: Those who disliked or envied Dion "called his gravity, 'pride'; his plainness and boldness in his oration, 'obstinacy'" and so on. Think of someone who has some characteristic you don't like or can't relate to, and see if you can find a positive side to them.

Lesson Three

Introduction

If you were bringing up a prince, how would you teach him to be a good and wise ruler? Dionysius I apparently did few or none of these things. He brought up his son to be self-centered, fearful, and useless; to have no love for learning, and to care only for entertainment. (It was a good way of making sure that he stayed in the background.)

Seeing this, Dion pushed young Dionysius to bring Plato back to Syracuse, and hoped that this attempt to plant seeds of wisdom would be more successful than the attempt previously made with his father.

Vocabulary

the liberal sciences: the study of philosophy, natural science, mathematics etc. such as Dion had studied with Plato

diffident: insecure

artificer: a skilled craftsperson or artisan

timorous: fearful

allow: admit (to something)

valiantest: bravest

marred: spoiled, ruined

cast away: destroyed

refer himself wholly…: put himself completely under his direction

God: Dryden translates this section "living after the likeness of the divine and glorious model of Being, out of obedience to whose control the general confusion is changed into the beautiful order of the universe…"

rehearsing these exhortations: preaching these sermons

vehement: strong, forceful

pliant: able to be shaped; impressionable

counterpoise: a factor that balances or neutralizes another

calumnies: lies, rumours

subvert: undermine, damage

over-licentious and imperious: also translated "dissolute and licentious"; unrestrained, high-handed, and (by implication) immoral

depose: dethrone

democratic: a form of government where a large number of people vote on decisions

aristocracy: in this context, the same as **oligarchy**, a form of government where a few elite rulers make the decisions

castle: see introductory notes for this study

decorum: good manners

concourse: crowd, gathering

People

Philistus (432-356 B.C.): (also spelled **Philistos**) a Syracusan historian. The Roman orator Cicero (much later) complimented him by calling him "the miniature Thucydides." It was partly through his wealth and influence that Dionysius I had been able to rise to power in Syracuse. He had been exiled during one of Dionysius' bouts of over-suspicion, but used that time to write the history of Sicily. He became extremely influential in the court of Dionysius II, and led much of the opposition to Dion.

Theodotes: a Syracusan general

Heracleides: (or **Heraclides**) Another Syracusan general. You might not notice him much here, but he will reappear in **Lesson Nine**.

Historic Occasions

366 B.C.: Dionysius II asserted his control over Syracuse

Reading

Part One

Now Dion well understood that he owed not his high position unto any goodwill or kindness, but to the mere necessities of the Usurper.

And, supposing that ignorance and want of education in Dionysius was the cause, he devised to put him into some honest trade or exercise, and teach him **the liberal sciences**, and to give him some knowledge of moral truths and reasonings, hoping he might thus lose his fear of virtuous living, and learn to take pleasure and delight in honest things. For Dionysius, of his own nature, was none of the worst sort of tyrant; but his father, fearing that if he came once to understand himself better, and converse with wise and reasonable men, he might enter into some design against him, and dispossess him of his power: he ever kept him locked up in a chamber, and would suffer no man to speak with him. Then the younger Dionysius having nothing else to do, gave himself to make little chariots, candlesticks, chairs, stools, and tables of wood.

For the elder Dionysius was so **diffident** and suspicious, and so continually on his guard against all men, that he would not so much as let his hair be trimmed with any barber's or hair-cutter's instruments, but made one of his **artificers** singe him with a live coal. Neither were his brother or his son allowed to come into his apartment in the dress they wore, but they, as all others, were stripped to their skins by some of the guard *[omission]*, and then put on other clothes before they were admitted into his presence.

[omission for length and content]

So **timorous** was he, and so miserable a slave to his fears; yet he had been very angry with Plato, because he would not **allow** him to be the **valiantest** man alive.

Part Two

Dion, as we said before, seeing the son clean **marred**, and in manner **cast away** for lack of good education, persuaded him the best he could to give himself unto study, and by the greatest entreaty he could possibly make, to pray Plato, the prince of all philosophers, to come into Sicily. And then when through his entreaty he were come, that he would **refer himself wholly unto him**, to the end that reforming his life by virtue and learning, and knowing **God** thereby (the best example that can be possible, and by whom all the whole world is ruled and governed, which otherwise were out of all order and confused), he should first obtain great happiness to himself, and consequently unto all his citizens also, who ever after through the temperance and justice of a father, would with goodwill do those things which they presently unwillingly did for the fear of a lord, and in doing this, from a tyrant he should come to be a king.

Dion oftentimes **rehearsing these exhortations** unto Dionysius, and otherwhile repeating some of the philosopher's sayings, he awoke in him a wonderful, and, as it were, a **vehement** desire to have Plato in his company, and to learn of him. So sundry letters came from Dionysius unto Athens, divers requests from Dion, and great entreaty made by certain philosophers, that prayed and persuaded Plato to come and obtain a hold upon this **pliant**, youthful soul, which his solid and weighty reasonings might steady, as it were, upon the seas of absolute power and authority. Plato, as he tells us himself, out of shame more than any other feeling, lest it should seem that he was all mere theory, and that of his own goodwill he would never venture into action, hoping withal, that if he could work a cure upon one man, the head and guide of the rest, he might remedy the distempers of the whole island of Sicily, yielded to their requests.

Part Three

But Dion's enemies fearing the change and alteration of Dionysius, they persuaded him to call **Philistus** the historian home again from banishment, who was a learned man, and at the same time of great experience in the ways of tyrants, and who might serve as a **counterpoise** to Plato and his philosophy.

[omission for length and content]

Philistus no sooner returned, but he stoutly began to defend the tyranny; and at the same time various **calumnies** and accusations against Dion were by others brought to the king, saying that he had held correspondence with **Theodotes** and **Heracleides** to **subvert** the government; as, doubtless, it is likely enough, that Dion had entertained hopes, by the coming of Plato, to bridle and lessen a little the **over-licentious and imperious** tyranny of Dionysius, and thereby to frame Dionysius a wise and righteous governor. But on the other side, if he saw he would not follow his counsel, and that he yielded not to his wise instructions, he then determined to **depose** him, and to bring the government of the commonwealth into the hands of the Syracusans: not that he approved a **democratic** government, but thought it altogether preferable to a tyranny, when a sound and good **aristocracy** could not be procured.

This was the state of affairs when Plato came into Sicily, where he was marvellously received and honoured by Dionysius. For when he landed on the shore, leaving his galley that brought him: there was ready for him one of the king's rich and sumptuous chariots to convey him to the **castle**: and the tyrant made sacrifice to give the gods thanks for his coming, for the great happiness which had befallen his government.

The citizens, also, began to entertain marvellous hopes of a speedy reformation, when they observed the modesty which now ruled in the banquets, and the general **decorum** which prevailed in all the court, their tyrant himself also behaving with gentleness and humanity in all their matters of business that came before him. There was a general passion for learning and philosophy, insomuch that the very palace, it is reported, was filled with sand and dust by the **concourse** of the students in mathematics who were working their problems there.

Narration and Discussion

Plutarch says that Dionysius I was powerful, but that he was a slave to his fears. How did this affect the upbringing of his son?

Why did certain people fear the alteration in Dionysius when he came under Plato's influence? Do you think the change will stick?

For older students and further thought: "From a tyrant he should come to be a king." What does this mean; wasn't Dionysius a king already? For a discussion of true kingship, look up Proverbs 31:3-9. Those who have read *The Once and Future King* (T.H. White) or *The Prydain Chronicles* (Lloyd Alexander) may find thoughts there as well.

Creative narration: Write, illustrate, or act out a scene between people in the royal court, discussing the strange change that has come over Dionysius, and how much they are now enjoying geometry; or write a letter from one character to another discussing the same thing.

Lesson Four

Introduction

The positive changes that had begun in Dionysius II caused him to wonder (out loud) if his rule over Syracuse was the best thing for the city. However, there were certain people who liked the government just the way it was; who felt threatened (as his father had) any time Dionysius began to think for himself; and who wanted very much to bring Dion's behind-the-scenes power to an end. Dion suddenly found himself accused of conspiring with Carthage, and banished to Greece, which actually turned out to be a great opportunity for him.

Plato was also sent home, but was then cajoled into returning. Dionysius could never seem to make up his mind about exactly what it was he wanted; but when he did demand something, there was no crossing him.

Vocabulary

conjectured: formed an opinion

hugger-mugger: secret

eloquence: power of speech

sophister: professor; professional thinker

hard usage: bad treatment

ensue: follow

some act which he should be sorry for: "Dion's stubbornness might force me to do something to him that I will regret later."

adherents: friends, supporters

petulant: sulky

humours: moods

In the meantime fell out war: Carthage, seeing that Syracuse was no longer protected by a strong ruler, attacked the city.

revenues: income from properties, business ventures, etc.

seat: country house; estate

infamy: reputation for evil

People

Callippus: a philosopher who will return to the story later

Speusippus: (or **Speusippos**) an Athenian philosopher who also happened to be the nephew of Plato.

Historic Occasions

366 B.C.: Dion banished from Syracuse

On the Map

Peloponnesus: the southern part of Greece, which included **Sparta**

Reading

Part One

Some few days after, it was the time of one of the Syracusan sacrifices; and when the priest, as he was wont, prayed for the long and safe continuance of the tyranny, Dionysius, it is said, as he stood by, cried out, "Leave off praying for evil upon us." This vexed Philistus and his party, who **conjectured** that if Plato, upon such brief acquaintance, had so far transformed and altered the young man's mind, longer converse and greater intimacy would give him such influence and authority that it would be impossible to withstand him.

And therefore they now began, not one by one, nor in **hugger-mugger**, but all of them with open mouth together, to accuse Dion: and said that it was easy to be seen how he charmed and enchanted Dionysius through Plato's **eloquence**, to make him willing to resign his government, because he (Dion) would transfer it to the hands of the children of his sister Aristomache. Others seemed to be offended because the Athenians, having previously come before into Sicily with a great army, could not win the city of Syracuse; but now by one only **sophister**, they (the Athenians) utterly destroyed and overthrew the empire of Dionysius, by persuading him to discharge the ten thousand soldiers he had about him for his guard, to forsake the four hundred galleys, the ten thousand horsemen, and as many more footmen, to go seek in the schools an unknown and imaginary bliss, and learn by mathematics how to be happy; while, in the meantime, the substantial enjoyments of absolute power, riches, and pleasure would be handed over to Dion and his sister's children.

By suchlike accusations and wicked tongues, Dionysius began first to mistrust Dion, and afterwards to be openly offended with him, and to frown upon him. In the meantime they brought letters Dion wrote secretly unto the governors of the city of Carthage, willing them that, when they would make peace with Dionysius, they should not talk with him unless he (Dion) stood by: assuring them that he would help them to set things in quietness, and that all should be well again.

When Dionysius had read these letters with Philistus, and had taken his advice and counsel what he should do, as Timaeus said, he deceived Dion under pretense of reconciliation, making as though he meant him no hurt, and saying that he would become friends again with him. So he brought Dion one day to the seaside under his castle, and showed him these letters, accusing him of having practised with the Carthaginians against him. And as Dion went about to make him answer, to clear himself, Dionysius would not hear him, but caused him to be taken up as he was, and put into a boat, and commanded the mariners to set him ashore upon the coast of Italy.

Part Two

When this was publicly known, and was thought very **hard usage**, there was much lamentation in the tyrant's own household on the part of the women; but the citizens of Syracuse encouraged themselves, expecting that for his sake some disturbance would **ensue**; which, together with the mistrust others would now feel, might occasion a general change and revolution in the state. Dionysius, seeing this, took alarm, and endeavoured to pacify the women and others of Dion's kindred and friends, assuring them that he had not banished him, but only sent him out of the way for a time, for fear of his own passion, which might be provoked someday by Dion's self-will into **some act which he should be sorry for**. He gave also two ships to his relations, with liberty to send into **Peloponnesus** for him whatever of his property or servants they thought fit. Dion was very rich, and had his house furnished with little less than royal splendour and magnificence. These valuables his friends packed up and conveyed to him, besides many rich presents which were sent him by the women and his **adherents**. So that, as far as wealth and riches went, he made a noble appearance among the Greeks, and they might judge, by the affluence of the exile, what was the power of the tyrant.

Part Three

But now concerning Plato: when Dion was exiled, Dionysius caused him (Plato) to be lodged in his castle, and by this means craftily placed, under cloak of friendship, an honourable guard about him, lest he should follow Dion, and declare to the world, on his behalf, how injuriously he had been dealt with. Howbeit Dionysius often frequenting his company (as a wild beast is made tame by company of man), he liked his talk so well, that he began to love the philosopher, but with such an affection as had something of the tyrant in it, requiring of Plato that he should, in return of his kindness, "love him only," and attend to him above all other men; being ready to put the whole realm into his hands, and all his forces, so that he would think better of him than of Dion. This extravagant affection was a great trouble to Plato, for it was accompanied with **petulant** and jealous **humours**, like the fond passions of those that are desperately in love. In a moment he would suddenly fall out with him, and straight again become friends, and pray him to pardon him.

In the meantime fell out war, and thereupon he sent Plato again away, promising him that the next spring he would recall Dion home, though in this he broke his word at once. Nevertheless, he sent him (Dion) his **revenues**, desiring Plato to excuse him as to the time appointed, because of the war; but, as soon as he had settled a peace, he would immediately send for Dion, whom in the meantime he prayed to have patience and not to attempt any stir or alteration against him, nor to speak evil of him among the Grecians.

This Plato sought to bring to pass, and brought Dion to study philosophy, and kept him in the Academy at Athens. Dion sojourned in the Upper Town of Athens, with **Callippus**, one of his acquaintance; but for his pleasure he bought a **seat** in the country, which afterwards, when he went into Sicily, he gave to **Speusippus**, who had been his most frequent companion while he was at Athens: Plato so arranging it, with the hope that Dion's austere temper might be softened by agreeable company, with an occasional mixture of seasonable mirth *[omission for length]*.

Dion went also to see several other cities, visiting the noblest and most statesmanlike persons in Greece, and joining in their recreations and entertainments in their times of festival. In all of this, no sort of vulgar ignorance, or tyrannic assumption, or luxuriousness was remarked in him; but, on the contrary, a great deal of temperance, generosity, and courage, and a well-becoming taste for reasoning and philosophic discourses. By which means he gained the love and admiration of all men, and in many cities had public honours decreed him; the Lacedaemonians making him a citizen of Sparta, without regard to the displeasure of Dionysius, though at that time he was aiding them in their wars against the Thebans *[omission for length]*.

Part Four

After some little time, Dionysius, envying Dion, and jealous of the favour and interest he had among the Grecians, put a stop upon his incomes, and no longer sent him his revenues, the which he gave to his receivers to keep. Furthermore, because he would clear himself of the **infamy** he had got amongst the philosophers for Plato's sake, he collected in his court many reputed learned men; and ambitiously desiring to surpass them in their debates, he was forced to make use, often incorrectly, of arguments he had picked up from Plato. And now he wished for his (Plato's) company again, repenting he had not made better use of it when he had it, and had given no greater heed to his admirable lessons. Like a tyrant, therefore, inconsiderate in his desires, headstrong and violent in whatever he took a will to, a sudden vehement desire took him in the head to have Plato again.

[Omission for length: Dionysius persuaded Plato to come back to Sicily.]

Narration and Discussion

Discuss what makes up a healthy friendship, and compare it to the Dionysius-Plato relationship. Why did Dionysius send Plato away? Why did he then want him back again?

How did Dion's manners change in Greece? What do you think his friendship with the Greeks could mean for him in the future?

For older students and further thought: In Mary Renault's novel *The Mask of Apollo*, Dion quotes Plato: "Philosophy is not a tool which can be passed about like a mason's rule; it is a fire struck from the glow of minds in search of truth." How might that apply to Dionysius?

Creative narration: Write or act out a scene in which Dion learns that his money has been cut off. How might he react?

Lesson Five

Introduction

Plato reluctantly accepted the invitation to return to Syracuse, but it didn't seem clear exactly what was expected of him. Dionysius welcomed him as a friend, offered him money, and even exempted him from the routine searches and palace metal detectors (so to speak). But when Plato wouldn't stop asking questions about Dion's absence, Dionysius (like his father) showed his vengeful side.

Vocabulary

affiance: faith

suffered: allowed

munificence: generosity

move him again of Dion: persuade him again to bring Dion back

covertly: secretly

talent of silver: A silver talent weighed 57 lb. (25.8 kg)

prognosticate: predict, foretell

he stood engaged for his safety…: Dionysius had guaranteed Plato's safety to Archytas, and therefore Archytas could formally request his return on the grounds that he was in danger.

dissuade him from it: persuade him not to do it

Dion was of great years: Dion would have been about fifty.

People

Aristippus: a philosopher from Cyrene, who had lived in Athens and studied with Socrates, but later lived much of his life in Syracuse

Helicon: a disciple of Plato, from the town of Cyzicus in Asia Minor

Archytas: a philosopher, mathematician, astronomer, and statesman, who lived in the city of Tarentum, in Italy

Timocrates: A Syracusan military leader who was sent to aid Sparta in 366 B.C. (at about the time that Dionysius II began his rule).

Eudemus the Cyprian: a philosopher and friend of Aristotle

Miltas the Thessalian: a member of the Platonic Academy

Reading

Part One

Now Plato being arrived in Sicily, he made Dionysius a great joyful man, and filled all Sicily again with great good hope: for they were all very desirous, and did what they could to make Plato overcome Philistus, and philosophy triumph over tyranny. The women of Dionysius' court did entertain Plato the best they could: but above all, Dionysius seemed to have a marvellous trust and **affiance** in him, more than in any other of all his friends. For he **suffered** Plato to come to him without searching of him, and oftentimes offered to give him a great sum of money: but Plato would take none of it. Therefore **Aristippus** the Cyrenaean being at that time in the tyrant's court in Sicily, said that Dionysius was very safe in his **munificence**: he gave little to those who were ready to take all they could get, and a great deal to Plato, who would accept of nothing.

After Dionysius had given Plato his welcome, he (Plato) began to **move him again of Dion**. Dionysius on the other side, at the first did use him with fine delays, but afterwards he showed himself angry indeed: and at length fell out with Plato, but yet so **covertly**, that others saw it not. For Dionysius endeavoured to conceal them, and, by other civilities and honourable usage, to draw him off from his affection to Dion. And for some time Plato himself was careful not to let anything of this dishonesty and breach of promise appear, but bore with it, and made as though he believed him.

While matters stood thus between them, and as they thought, they were unobserved and undiscovered, **Helicon** the Cyzicenian, one of Plato's followers, foretold an eclipse of the sun, which happened according to his prediction: for which he was much admired by the tyrant, and rewarded with a **talent of silver**. Then Aristippus, sporting with other philosophers, said he could tell them of a stranger thing to happen than that. So when they prayed him to tell them what it was: "I do **prognosticate**," said he, "that Plato and Dionysius will be enemies ere it be long."

Part Two

At length, Dionysius sold all Dion's goods, and kept the money himself; and he removed Plato from an apartment he had in the gardens of the palace to lodgings among the guards he kept in pay, who from the first had hated Plato, and sought opportunity to kill him, supposing he (Plato) advised Dionysius to leave his tyranny and disband his soldiers.

When **Archytas** understood the danger Plato was in, he immediately sent a galley with messengers to demand him of Dionysius: alleging that **he stood engaged for his safety, upon the confidence of which Plato had come to Sicily**. Dionysius, to excuse himself, and to show that he was not angry with him at his departure from him, he made him all the great cheer and feasts he could, and so sent him home with great shows of goodwill. One day among the rest, he said unto Plato: "I am afraid, Plato," said he, "that thou wilt speak evil of me, when thou art among thy friends and companions in the Academy." Then Plato smiling, answered him again: "The gods forbid that they should have such scarcity of matter in the Academy, as that they must needs talk of thee." Thus was Plato's return, as it is reported, although that which he himself writeth agrees not much with this report.

Part Three

These things went to Dion's heart, so that shortly after he showed himself an open enemy unto Dionysius, but especially when he heard how he had handled his wife; on which matter Plato, also, had had some confidential correspondence with Dionysius. Thus it was. After Dion's banishment, Dionysius, when he sent Plato back, had desired him to ask Dion privately if he would be averse to his wife's marrying another man *[omission for content]*. Soon afterwards, Dionysius forced Dion's wife (and his own sister) Arete, against her will, to marry **Timocrates**, one of his favourites *[omission for content]*.

Dion from thenceforth disposed himself altogether unto war, against Plato's counsel and advice: who did his best endeavour to **dissuade him from it**, both for the respect of Dionysius' good entertainment he had given him, as also for that **Dion was of great years**. Howbeit on the other side, Speusippus and his other friends did provoke him unto it, and did persuade him to deliver Sicily from the slavery and bondage of the tyrant, the which held up her hands unto him, and would receive him with great love and goodwill. For whilst Plato lay at Syracuse, Speusippus keeping the citizens company more than Plato did, he knew their minds better than he. For at the first they were afraid to open themselves unto him (Speusippus), and frankly to speak what they thought, mistrusting he was a spy unto the tyrant, sent amongst them to feel their minds: but within a short time they began to trust him, and were all of one mind, for they prayed and persuaded Dion to come, and not to care otherwise for bringing of ships, soldiers nor horses with him; but only to hire a ship, and to lend the Sicilians his person and name against Dionysius.

This information from Speusippus encouraged Dion, who, concealing his real purpose, employed his friends privately to raise what men they could; and many statesmen and philosophers were assisting him, as, for instance, **Eudemus the Cyprian** and **Miltas the Thessalian**. But of all that were banished by Dionysius, who were not fewer than a thousand, five and twenty only joined in the enterprise; the rest were afraid and abandoned it.

Narration and Discussion

Plato returned to Syracuse because Dionysius had promised, in return, to bring Dion out of his banishment. Do you think he expected Dionysius to keep his promise?

Was Dion justified in planning war against Dionysius? What were the reasons for and against it?

For further thought: One of the philosophers predicted a solar eclipse. Another foretold that Dionysius and Plato would become enemies. Both predictions were made by recognizing conditions that would make an event possible or likely to happen, and this interest in "why" was of great interest to Greek philosophers.

As part of the AmblesideOnline curriculum, you may be reading *Madam How and Lady Why* by Charles Kingsley, which examines these questions. The idea of cause and effect is also explored in literature, from great novels down to picture books. Choose one historical event or natural phenomenon, and explain the chain of events which caused it. Alternatively, try to predict something that will happen, based on your understanding of the conditions necessary for it to occur.

Creative narration: Plato, after his rescue by Archytas, would have returned to Athens as soon as he could. Write or act out a meeting between Plato and his friends at the Academy, or between Plato and Dion (who was living in Athens at that time).

Lesson Six

Introduction

Over the next year or so, Dion prepared for war against Dionysius by hiring as many mercenary soldiers as he could; his plan was to take them to Sicily and raise up a Syracusan army as well. The soldiers were not enthusiastic at first, believing that this was just a private grudge match between Dion and the tyrant. But when Dion promised them that they would be captains over the Syracusans, and they realized that he had the support of wealthy and powerful friends, they seemed to catch the spirit of the thing; especially with the help of some "good omens" like an eclipse.

Vocabulary

animate: bring to life, push into action

muster-master: an officer who takes account of troops and their equipment

arbitrary government: This can refer to a government that is set over people without their agreeing to it; but, more specifically, it describes a government without limits, run at the whims of those in power.

Etesian winds: north winds of the Aegean Sea

in all their arms and accoutrements: carrying their weapons and wearing their uniforms

libations: "drink offerings"; religious rituals involving the pouring out of wine to a deity

God: Dryden, "the divine powers"

pinnaces: small boats. Dryden, however, translates this "galleys."

looking out for them: It is important to note (if there is any question!) that Philistus was not attempting to ensure their safe return, but to prevent it.

luff: sailing term: to set the helm in such a way as to bring the head of the vessel into the wind

tempest: storm

in the dominion of the Carthaginians: Carthage ruled part of Sicily at that time, and Minoa was within their territory.

People

Miltas the soothsayer: see previous lesson

Historic Occasions

357 B.C.: Dion's fleet sailed for Sicily

On the Map

Zacynthe: (in Greek, *Zakynthos*) an island off the west coast of Greece

Iapygia (Iapygians): also called Apulia (Apulians); the region of Italy which occupies the heel of Italy's "boot"

Pachynus: now called Capo Passero or Cape Passaro, on the southeastern side of Sicily

Libya: a country of northern Africa, on the Mediterranean Sea

Great Syrtis: or the Gulf of Sidra, on the northern coast of Libya

Minoa: Heraclea Minoa, a city on the south coast of Sicily

Reading

Part One

The place where Dion's forces were appointed to meet was the isle of **Zacynthe**, where a small force of eight hundred men came together, all of them, however, persons already distinguished in plenty of previous hard service, their bodies well trained and practiced, and their experience and courage amply sufficient to **animate** and embolden to action the numbers whom Dion expected to join him in Sicily.

Yet these hired soldiers, the first time that they understood it was to go into Sicily, to make war with Dionysius, they were amazed at the first, and misliked the journey, accusing Dion, that, hurried on like a madman by mere passion and despair, he rashly threw both himself and them into certain ruin. Nor were they less angry with their commanders and **muster-masters** that they had not in the beginning let them know the design. But after Dion in his address to them had set forth the unsafe and weak condition of **arbitrary government**, and declared that he carried them rather for commanders than soldiers, the citizens of Syracuse and rest of the Sicilians having been long ready for a revolt; and when, after him also Alcimenes (a companion with him in this war, and the chiefest man of all the Achaians, both for nobility and estimation) did speak unto them in like manner, then they were all contented to go whither they would lead them.

It was now the middle of summer, and the **Etesian winds** blowing steadily on the seas, the moon was at the full, when Dion prepared a magnificent sacrifice to Apollo; and with great solemnity marched his soldiers to the temple **in all their arms and accoutrements**. And after the sacrifice was done, he made them a feast in the racecourse of the Zacynthians. There the tables were laid, and the soldiers wondered to see the great state and magnificence of the great number of pots of gold and silver, and such other furniture and preparation exceeding a private man's wealth; then they thought with themselves, that a man being so old, and lord of so great a good, would not attempt things of such danger without good ground, and great assurance of his friends' aid and help.

But just after the **libations** were made, and the accompanying prayers offered, suddenly the moon eclipsed. This was no wonder to Dion, who understood the revolutions of eclipses, and the way in which the moon is overshadowed and the earth interposed between her and the sun. But because the soldiers that were afraid and astonished withal, stood in need of some comfort and encouragement, **Miltas the soothsayer** standing up in the midst amongst them, said unto them:

> "My fellow soldiers: be of good cheer, and assure yourselves that we shall prosper: for **God** doth foreshow us by this sight we see, that some one of the chiefest things now in highest place and dignity shall be eclipsed. And at this present time what thing carrieth greater glory and fame, than the tyranny of Dionysius? Therefore you must think, that so soon as you arrive in Sicily, yourselves shall put out his light and glory."

This interpretation of the eclipse of the moon, did Miltas the soothsayer make, before all the whole company.

But touching the swarm of bees that lighted on the deck of Dion's ship, Miltas told him and his friends privately that he was afraid his acts which should fall out famous and glorious, should last but a while, and flourishing a few days, would straight consume away.

[Omission: strange omens were noticed also by the soothsayers of Dionysius.]

Part Two

So Dion's soldiers were embarked into two great ships of burden, and another third ship that was not very great; and two **pinnaces** with thirty oars followed them. For their armour and weapons, beside those the soldiers had, he carried two thousand targets, a great number of bows and arrows, of darts, of pikes; and plenty of victuals: that they should lack nothing all the time they were upon the sea, considering that their journey stood altogether at the courtesy of the winds and sea, and for that they were afraid to land; and Philistus, they had been told, was in **Iapygia** with a fleet, **looking out for them**.

So having a pleasant gale of wind, they sailed the space of twelve days together, and the thirteen day they came to the foreland of Sicily, called **Pachynus**. There the pilot thought it best they should land presently: for if they willingly **luffed** into the sea, and lost that point, they were sure they should lose also many nights and days in vain in the midst of the sea, it being then summer time; and the wind at the south. But Dion being afraid to land so near his enemies, he was desirous to go further, and so sailed on past Pachynus.

Then the north wind rose so big and great, that with great violence it drove back their ships from the coast of Sicily. Furthermore, lightning and thunder mingled withal (because it was at that time when the star Arcturus rises), it made so terrible a **tempest**, and poured down such a sore shower of rain upon them, that all the mariners were amazed withal, and knew not whither the wind would drive them: till that suddenly they saw the storm had cast them upon the isle of Cercina (which is on the coast of **Libya**), just where it is most craggy and dangerous to run upon. Upon the cliffs there they escaped narrowly being forced and staved to pieces; but, labouring hard at their oars, with much difficulty they kept clear until the storm ceased. Then, lighting by chance upon a vessel, they understood they were upon the Heads, as it is called, of the **Great Syrtis**; and when they were now again marvellous angry that the sea was calm, there rose a little south wind from the land, although they least looked for any such wind at that time, and little thinking it would so have changed: but seeing the wind rise bigger and bigger, they packed on all the sails they had, and making their prayers unto the gods they crossed the sea, and sailed from the coast of Libya directly unto Sicily.

And, running steady before the wind, the fifth day they arrived at **Minoa**, a little town of Sicily, **in the dominion of the Carthaginians**, of which Synalus, an acquaintance and friend of Dion's, happened at that time to be governor; who, not knowing it was Dion and his fleet, endeavoured to hinder his men from landing; but they rushed on shore with their swords in their hands, not slaying any of their opponents (for this Dion had forbidden, because of his friendship with the Carthaginians); but forced them to retreat; and, following close, pressed in a body with them into the place, and took it.

When both the captains met, and that they had spoken together, Dion redelivered the town into Synalus' hands again, without any hurt or violence offered him. Synalus on the other side did endeavour himself all he could to make much of the soldiers, and supplied Dion with what he wanted.

Narration and Discussion

Creative narration: Retell some part of this lesson from the viewpoint of one of the soldiers, in any format you choose (conversation at the dinner party, or a news interview after their arrival at Minoa).

Preparation for the next lesson: Lessons Seven to **Eleven** describe the siege of the Syracusan "castle." But which castle are we talking about? Please read the introductory notes for this study, as there were two sites involved at different times

To help with both readings and narrations, it would be useful to set up a model of the city and the fortress on the island of Ortygia, to show the action and also to keep track of particular characters. The people don't have to be realistic: toothpicks with nametags attached will work. You will also want a few generic figures to represent soldiers on each side. Toy ships or buildings can be put to use, but materials such as construction bricks, natural materials, or household objects are fine too (a box could represent the castle).

Lesson Seven

Dion and his army, having landed on Sicily, and feeling a little tired and "seabeaten," heard news that instantly re-energized them: Dionysius had suddenly found it necessary to be away from Syracuse. Rumours of their march towards Syracuse reached Timocrates; but his panic-stricken letter to Dionysius ended up being eaten by mistake. The coincidences and good omens continued to pile up until Timocrates fled in fear, and Dion marched in to liberate the city.

Vocabulary

would not: That is, they would not stay and rest for a few days, preferring to march on Syracuse while they had the opportunity.

superfluous: extra

mutton: sheep

Epipolae: the hill where the castle was located

their towns: Lentini and Campania

ten furlongs: 1.25 miles (2 km)

in their best gowns: Dryden, "clad all in white"

the populace: the common people, the masses (sometimes the mob)

popular government: a state governed by or belonging to the people

People

Megacles: (also spelled **Megakles**) the brother of Dion

Callippus the Athenian: see **Lesson Four**

Historic Occasions

357 B.C.: Dionysius II deposed by Dion

On the Map

Agrigento (Agrigentines), Gela (Geloans), Camarina (Camarinians): cities on the south coast of Sicily

Rhegium, Caulonia: two cities in the region of Calabria

Campania (Campanians): a region of southwestern Italy

Leontini (Leontines): Now called Lentini; a city southeast of Syracuse

river of Anapus: The Anapo river in Sicily

Reading

Part One

Dion's soldiers were most of all encouraged by the happy accident of Dionysius' absence at their arrival; for it appeared that, not many days before, he had gone into Italy with eighty ships. Therefore when Dion willed them to remain there a few days to refresh themselves, because they had been so sore seabeaten a long time together, they themselves **would not**, they were so glad to embrace the occasion offered them, and prayed Dion to lead them forthwith to Syracuse. Dion left all his **superfluous** armour and provision in the hands of Synalus; and, praying him to send them to him when time served, he marched directly to Syracuse.

The first that came in to him upon his march were two hundred horsemen of the **Agrigentines** who were settled near Ecnomum; and, after them, the **Geloans**. The rumour of their coming ran straight to Syracuse. Thereupon Timocrates that had married Arete (Dion's wife, the sister of Dionysius), and who was the principle man among his friends now remaining in the city, immediately dispatched a courier to Dionysius, with letters announcing Dion's arrival; while he himself took all possible care to prevent any stir or tumult in the city, where all were in great excitement; but because they were uncertain whether this rumour was true or false, being afraid, every man was quiet.

Now there chanced a strange misfortune unto the messenger that carried the letters unto Dionysius. For after he had passed the strait, and was arrived in **Rhegium**, making haste to come to the city of **Caulonia**, where Dionysius was, he met by the way one of his acquaintance that carried a **mutton** but newly sacrificed. This good fellow gave him a piece of it, and the messenger spurred away with all the speed he could possible. But when he had ridden the most part of the night, he was so weary and drowsy for lack of sleep, that he was driven to lie down. So he lay down upon the ground, in a wood hard by the highway. The savour of this flesh brought a wolf to him, that carried away the flesh and the bag it was wrapped in, in which also were the letters to Dionysius.

When he awoke out of his sleep, and saw that his bag was gone, sought for it up and down a great while; and, not finding it, resolved not to go to the king without his letters, but to conceal himself, and keep out of the way. Dionysius, therefore, came to hear of the war of Sicily from other hands, and that a good while after.

Part Two

In the meantime, the **Camarinians** came and joined with Dion's army, in the highway towards Syracuse: and still there came unto him also a great number of the Syracusans that were up in arms, which were got into the field. On the other side, certain **Campanians** and **Leontines**, which were got into the **Epipolae** with Timocrates, of purpose to keep it, upon a false rumour Dion gave out (and which came unto them) that he would first go against **their towns**, they forsook Timocrates, and went to take order to defend their own goods. Dion understanding that, being lodged with his army in a place called Macrae, he presently removed his camp being dark night, and marched forward till he came unto the **river of Anapus**, which is not from the city above **ten furlongs** off: and there staying a while, he sacrificed unto the river, and made his prayer, and worshipped the rising of the sun.

At the selfsame instant also, the soothsayers came and told him that the gods did promise him assured victory. And the soldiers also, seeing Dion wear a garland of flowers on his head, which he had taken for the ceremony of the sacrifice, one and all crowned themselves with garlands. There were about five thousand men that had joined his forces in their march; who, though but ill-provided, with such weapons as came next to hand, made up by zeal and courage for the want of better arms; and when Dion commanded them to march, for joy they ran, and encouraged one another with great cries, to show themselves valiant for recovery of their liberty.

Part Three

Now for them that were within Syracuse itself, the noblemen and chief citizens went to receive them at the gates **in their best gowns**. **The populace** set upon all that were of Dionysius' party, and principally searched for those they called "setters" or "informers," a number of wicked and hateful wretches who made it their business to go up and down the city, thrusting themselves into all companies, that they might inform Dionysius what men said, and how they stood affected. These men were they that had their payment first of all, for they killed them with dry blows, beating them to death with staves.

When Timocrates could not enter into the castle with them that kept it, he took to horseback, and fled out of the city, filling all the places where he came with fear and confusion, magnifying the amount of Dion's forces, because it should not seem that, for fear of a trifle, he had forsaken the city.

In the meantime, Dion came on towards the city with his men, and was come so near that they might see him plainly from the city, marching foremost of all, in a rich suit of arms, having his brother **Megacles** on his right hand of him, and **Callippus the Athenian** on the left hand, crowned with garlands of flowers: and after him also there followed a hundred soldiers that were strangers, chosen for his guard about him, and the rest came marching after in good order of battle, being led by their captains. The Syracusans looked on and welcomed them, as if they believed the whole to be a sacred and religious procession, to celebrate the solemn entrance, after an absence of forty-eight years, of liberty and **popular government**.

Narration and Discussion

Tell about Dion's day of glory. Could anyone (besides the soothsayers) have predicted this?

Why does Plutarch say that the tale-bearers were hateful to the gods and men? Why did they receive the first and most violent retaliation for their actions? Should such people have been forgiven?

Creative narration: Use the model you built to narrate this lesson.

Lesson Eight

Introduction

The conflict between Dion and Dionysius was much like a game of chess. Dion made his opening move; Dionysius (who had returned to Syracuse) considered it and made a countermove; Dion mustered his army and forced a retreat; but Dionysius, devious as always, tried to create suspicion against Dion.

Vocabulary

Acradina, Epipolae: sections (neighbourhoods) of Syracuse

Pentapyla: or Pentapylon; five towers protecting the castle

soothsayers and prognosticators: those who predicted the future

sumptuous: splendid

turn and declination of Fortune: change from good luck to bad

returned by sea to the castle of Syracuse: At first Dionysius was merely protecting himself on Ortygia, but, shortly afterwards, he was besieged by the Syracusans.

they should pay no more subsidies and taxes: not that they should not pay their taxes, but that there would be no more taxes required

procuring oblivion for the past: letting bygones be bygones

For those that were sent him…: Some sources include Dion with the prisoners, but Plutarch does not say that.

sally: a sudden charge out of a besieged fort or city

mina: a unit of money

People

Timonides: Timonides of Leukas, military officer and historian

Reading

Part One

When Dion was come into the city by the Menitid Gate, and, having by sound of trumpet quieted the noise of the people, he caused proclamation to be made that Dion and Megacles, who were come to put down the tyranny, did set all the Syracusans at liberty, and all the other Sicilians also, from the bondage and subjection of the tyrant; and because Dion himself was desirous to speak unto the people, he went up through the **Acradina**. The Syracusans, all the streets thorough as he passed by, had on either hand of him prepared sacrifices, and set up tables, and cups upon them: and as he passed by their houses, they cast flowers and fruits on him, and made prayers unto him, as if he had been a god.

Now under the castle and the **Pentapyla** there was a sun-dial, which Dionysius had set up, and it was of a good pretty height. Dion got up upon it, and from thence made his oration to the people that were gathered round about him, exhorting and persuading his countrymen to do their endeavour to recover their liberty again, and to maintain it. They being in a marvellous joy withal, and desirous to please Dion, did choose him and his brother Megacles their generals, with absolute power and authority. Afterwards also, by the consent of Dion himself and his brother, and at their requests in like manner, they chose twenty other captains, of the which the most part of them had been banished by the tyrant, and were returned again with Dion. The **soothsayers and prognosticators** liked it well, and said it was a good sign for Dion, that he trod that **sumptuous** building and workmanship of the tyrant under his feet, when he made his oration; but because it was a sun-dial on which he stood when he was made general, they expressed some fears that the great actions he had performed might be subject to change, and admit some rapid **turn and declination of Fortune**.

Part Two

After this, Dion having taken the **Epipolae**, he set all the citizens at liberty which were kept there as prisoners in captivity by the tyrant, and environed the castle roundabout with a wall. Within seven days after, Dionysius **returned by sea to the castle of Syracuse**, and therewithal also came the carts laden with armour and weapons to Syracuse, the which Dion had left with Synalus, which Dion caused to be distributed among the citizens of Syracuse that had none. Others did furnish themselves as well as they could, and showed that they had courage and goodwill to fight for the maintenance and defense of their liberty.

In the meantime, Dionysius sent ambassadors, first unto Dion privately, to try what terms they could make with him. But Dion would not hear them, but bade them tell the Syracusans openly what they had to say, being men that were free, and enjoyed liberty. Then the ambassadors spoke on behalf of the tyrant, unto the people of Syracuse, promising them with mild and gentle words that **they should pay no more subsidies and taxes**, but very little, and should be no more troubled with wars, other than such as they themselves should like of. The Syracusans laughed at these offers, and Dion returned answer to the envoys, that Dionysius must not think to treat with them upon any other terms but resigning the government; which if he would actually do, he would not forget how nearly he was related to him, or be wanting to assist him in **procuring oblivion for the past**, and whatever else was reasonable and just.

Dionysius liked very well of this good offer, and therefore sent his ambassadors again to pray the Syracusans that they would appoint some amongst them to come to the castle, to talk with him for the benefit and commodity of the commonwealth, that he might hear what they would allege, and they also what answer he would make. Dion chose certain men, whom he sent unto him.

Now there ran a rumour in the city among the Syracusans, which came from the castle, that Dionysius would willingly, of himself, rather than by reason of Dion's coming, depose himself of the tyranny. But this was but a false alarm, and crafty fetch of Dionysius, to entrap the Syracusans by. **For those that were sent him from the city**, he kept them prisoners every man of them; and one morning having made his soldiers drink wine lustily, which he kept in pay to guard his person, he sent them with great fury to assault the wall the Syracusans had built against the castle. The attack was quite unexpected, and the barbarians set to work boldly with loud cries to pull down the cross-wall, and assailed the Syracusans so furiously that they were not able to maintain their post. Only a party of Dion's hired soldiers, on first taking the alarm, advanced to the rescue; neither did they at first know what to do, or how to employ the aid they brought, not being able to hear the commands of their officers, amidst the noise and confusion of the Syracusans, who fled from the enemy and ran in among them, breaking through their ranks, until Dion, seeing none of his orders could be heard, resolved to let them see by example what they ought to do, and charged into the thickest of the enemy.

Part Three

All about him there was a cruel and bloody fight. For his enemies knew him as well as his own men, and they all ran upon him with great cries. Though his time of life was no longer that of the bodily strength and agility for such a combat, still his determination and courage were sufficient to maintain him against all that attacked him. Yet he had his hand also thrust thorough with a pike; his body armour also had been much battered, and was scarcely any longer serviceable to protect him, either against missiles or blows hand-to-hand. Many spears and javelins had passed into it through the shield, and, on these being broken back, he fell to the ground, but was immediately rescued and carried off by his soldiers.

The command-in-chief he left to **Timonides**, and, mounting a horse, he rode about the city, rallying the Syracusans that fled; and ordering a detachment of the foreign soldiers out of Acradina, where they were posted on guard, he brought them as a fresh reserve, eager for battle, upon the tired and failing enemy, who were already well inclined to give up their design.

For having hoped at their first **sally** to take the whole city, when beyond their expectation they found themselves engaged with bold and practiced fighters, they fell back towards the castle. And the Grecian soldiers on the other side, perceiving they gave back, they came the faster upon them, so that they were compelled to turn their backs, and were driven within their walls, after they had slain seventy-four of Dion's men, and lost a great number of their own. This was a noble victory, and therefore the Syracusans gave the soldiers that were strangers a hundred silver **minas**, in reward for their good service: and they gave Dion, their general, a crown of gold.

Narration and Discussion

Dion had been sent on many diplomatic missions in his lifetime, and was certainly able to negotiate and compromise when necessary. Why then was he unwilling to accept anything other than full surrender?

How did Dion show leadership in the battle described here? What personal difficulties did he have to ignore?

Creative narration #1: Write this passage as a series of news headlines.

Creative narration #2: Use the model you built to narrate this lesson.

Lesson Nine

Introduction

Dion was now the Syracusan general or *archon*, with absolute power and authority (although the siege of the castle continued, with Dion's relatives being held there as hostages). Certain people grumbled about his apparent grab for power, having forgotten who led the liberation of Syracuse; and their suspicions were increased with the arrival of a letter from Dionysius (addressed to Dion, but read to everyone), begging him to keep the power of Syracuse in his own hands rather than hand it over to the less-capable public. Dion's enemies began to make noises about the need for fresh leadership.

Vocabulary

companion-in-arms: fellow soldier

plausible: credible, believable

entreaty: humble request

magnanimity: noble spirit

withstood all his dearest interests: set aside personal interests (such as protecting family members)

invincible necessity: pressing need

to have the better hand of him: to be in a place of advantage

generalissimo, chieftain general: *archon*; the one highest in command

repealed: cancelled

People

Heracleides: Mentioned briefly in **Lesson Three**. Heracleides was an admiral who had fled to the Peloponnesus (probably along with Dion) after being suspected of conspiring to overthrow the government. He had helped plan the expedition back to Syracuse, but remained behind, possibly (as Plutarch says) because he and Dion had some disagreement; other sources say he was busy gathering soldiers and/or was delayed by bad weather.

Philistus: See **Lesson Three**

Apollocrates: the son of Dionysius

Historic Occasions

356 B.C.: Dionysius left Syracuse

Reading

Part One

After this, there came heralds from Dionysius, bring Dion letters from the women of his family, and one addressed outside, "to his father, from Hipparinus"; this was the name of Dion's son, though Timaeus says he was, from his mother Arete's name, called Aretaeus. But in such matters, methinks Timonides is better to be credited, because he was his friend and **companion-in-arms**.

All the other letters that were sent were openly read before the assembly of the Syracusans, and did only concern requests of these women unto Dion. The Syracusans would not have the supposed letter of his son to be openly read: but Dion, against their minds opened it, and found that it was Dionysius' letter, who by words made the direction of it unto Dion, but in effect he spoke unto the Syracusans; and so worded that, under a **plausible** justification of himself and **entreaty** to him, means were taken for rendering him suspected by the people.

First of all he reminded him of the good service he had formerly done the usurping government; it added threats to his dearest relations, his sister, son, and wife, if he did not comply with the contents; also passionate demands mingled with lamentations. But that which most moved Dion of all other was, that he (Dionysius) required him not to destroy the tyranny, but rather to take it for himself; and not to set them at liberty that hated him, and would always remember the mischief he had done unto them: and that he would himself take upon him to be lord, saving by that means the lives of his family and friends.

Part Two

When this letter was read, the Syracusans were not, as they should have been, transported with admiration at the unmovable constancy and **magnanimity** of Dion, who **withstood all his dearest interests** to be true to virtue and justice, but, on the contrary, they saw in this their reason for fearing and suspecting that he lay under an **invincible necessity** to be favourable to Dionysius; and they began, therefore, to look out for other leaders, and the rather because to their great joy they received the news that **Heracleides** was on his way.

This Heracleides was one of them that had been banished, a good soldier and captain, and well esteemed of for the charge and office he bore under the tyrants; yet a man of no constant purpose, of a fickle temper, and least of all to be relied upon when he had to act with a colleague in any honourable command. He had fallen out with Dion in Peloponnesus, and had resolved, upon his own means, with what ships and soldiers he had, to make an attack upon Dionysius.

So he arrived at length at Syracuse, with seven galleys and three other ships, where he found Dionysius again shut up into his castle with a wall, and the Syracusans also **to have the better hand of him**. Then he began to curry favour with the common people all the ways he could possibly devise, having by nature a certain pleasing manner to win the common people, which seek nothing else but to be flattered. Furthermore, he found it the easier for him to win them, because the people did already mislike Dion's severity, as a man too severe and cruel to govern a commonwealth. For they had now their will so much, and were grown so strong-headed, because they saw themselves the stronger, that they would be flattered (as commonly the people be in free cities, where they only be lords, and do rule) before they had in reality secured a popular government.

Therefore, getting together in an irregular assembly, they chose Heracleides their admiral; but when Dion came forward, and told them that conferring this trust upon Heracleides was in effect to withdraw that which they had granted him, for he was no longer their **generalissimo** if another had the command of the navy: they **repealed** their order, and, though much against their wills, cancelled the new appointment. When this business was over, Dion invited Heracleides to his house, and pointed out to him, in gentle terms, that he had not acted wisely or well to quarrel with him upon a point of honour, at a time when the least false step might be the ruin of all; and then, calling a fresh assembly of the people, he there named Heracleides admiral, and prevailed with the citizens to allow him a life-guard, as he himself had.

Heracleides outwardly seemed to honour Dion, and confessed openly that he was greatly bound unto him, and was always at his heels very lowly, being ready at his commandment: but in the meantime, secretly he enticed the common people to rebel, and to stir up those whom he knew meet men to like of change. Whereby he procured Dion such trouble, and brought him into such perplexity, that he knew not well what way to take. For if he (Dion) gave them advice to let Dionysius quietly come out of the castle, then they accused him; and said he did it to save his life. If on the other side, because he would not trouble them, he continued the siege still, and did establish nothing, then they thought he did it of purpose to draw out the wars in length, because he might the longer time remain their **chieftain general**, and so to keep the citizens longer in fear.

[omission for length and content]

Part Three

The Syracusans were as jealous as before of Dion's soldiers, and the rather because the war was now carried on principally by sea, Philistus being come from Iapygia with a great fleet to assist Dionysius. They supposed, therefore, that there would be no longer need of the soldiers, who were all landsmen and armed accordingly; these were rather, indeed, they thought, in a condition to be protected by themselves, who were seamen, and had their power in their shipping.

Their good opinion of themselves was also much enhanced by an advantage they got in an engagement by sea, in which they took Philistus prisoner, and used him in a barbarous and cruel manner.

[Omission for length and content. The historian Ephorus says that Philistus took his own life after the battle.]

After Philistus' death, Dionysius sent to Dion, offering to surrender the castle, all the arms, provisions, and garrison soldiers, with full pay for them for five months; demanding in return that he might have safe conduct to go unmolested into Italy, to take the pleasure of the fruits of the country called Gyarta, which was within the territory of Syracuse, reaching from the seaside to the middle of the country. Dion refused this offer, and referred him to the Syracusans. They, supposing they should easily take Dionysius alive, would not hear the ambassadors speak, but turned them away.

Dionysius, seeing no other remedy, left the castle in the hands of his eldest son **Apollocrates**, and, having a lusty gale of wind, he secretly put on board his ships the persons and the property that he set most value upon, and made his escape, undiscovered by the admiral and his fleet.

[omission for length; see the synopsis at the beginning of ***Lesson Ten****]*

Narration and Discussion

Plutarch says that Dion "withstood all his dearest interests to be true to virtue and justice." Do you agree? Was he most concerned about the well-being of Syracuse, or was he trying to keep all the power for himself (and away from Heracleides)?

Most of what we know about Heracleides comes only from this story, and as Plutarch tends to take Dion's side of matters, it may be a bit biased. Write or act out an interview with Heracleides, allowing him to tell his side of the story.

For older students and further thought: In this passage Plutarch says that the "common people" only want to be flattered; that they don't know what to do with power when they get it; and that they are led by emotion rather than wisdom. Do you agree with this judgment?

Creative narration: Use the model you built to narrate this lesson.

Lesson Ten

Introduction

The following is a condensed version of the events omitted between **Lessons Nine** and **Ten**.

Dion's enemies among the Syracusans tried to persuade his Peloponnesian soldiers to desert him, but they refused, and marched out of town with Dion protected in the midst of them. And the Syracusans followed them, planning to attack. At first there was no battle; Dion tried to "pacify their fury and tumult," but was unsuccessful. He forbade his men to attack first, but they did rattle their weapons and yell in a way that scared the Syracusans back into their city. Then, feeling ashamed of their cowardice, they marched out once again and overtook Dion's army. Dion was much less patient with them this time and told his men to fight back as they wished. It didn't take much of a fight to send them scurrying for home again.

Dion marched his mercenaries to the city of the **Leontines**, and a Sicilian congress sat in judgment over the Syracusan situation. Plutarch says, "it was judged that the Syracusans were to blame. Howbeit they would not stand to the judgment of their **confederates**, for they were now grown proud and careless, because they were governed by no man, but had captains that studied to please them, and were afraid also to displease them."

And with that, we arrive at the opening scene of **Lesson Ten**, as the Syracusans (without the help of Dion) besieged the island fortress; and some unexpected help arrived for Dionysius.

Vocabulary

confederates: friends, allies

works: siegeworks; constructions built by those besieging a place

barbarians: In other *Lives*, the word "barbarians" refers specifically to Persians; but in this case it seems a general term for foreign soldiers.

sacked: destroyed, plundered

garboil: turmoil

seditious governors: those attempting to end Dion's leadership

let Dion alone: cancel the request for him to come and help

Dion marched very softly at his ease: Some were pleading with Dion to hurry to Syracuse, others were pleading with him not to come at all; so he compromised and marched slowly.

sacked the city: The first "sacking" (see above) had been bad, but this one was even worse.

strait and desperate case: tight situation

mortal malice: deep hatred

sixty furlongs: about 7.5 miles (12 km)

People

Nypsius the Neapolitan: We do not have further information on him.

On the Map

Leontini (Leontines): see **Lesson Seven**

Reading

Part One

After that, there arrived certain galleys of Dionysius at Syracuse, under the command of **Nypsius the Neapolitan**, which brought victuals and money to help them that were besieged within the castle. The Syracusans fought him, had the better, and took four of his ships; but they made very ill use of their good success. For they, having nobody to command nor rule them, employed all their joy in rioting and banqueting, taking so little care and regard to their business that now, when they thought the castle was sure their own, they almost lost their city. For Nypsius, seeing the citizens in this general disorder, spending day and night in their drunken singing and reveling, and their commanders well-pleased with the frolic, or at least not daring to try and give any orders to men in their drink, took advantage of this opportunity, made a sally, and stormed their **works**; and, having made his way through these, let his **barbarians** loose upon the city, and commanded them to do with them they met, what they would or could.

The Syracusans quickly saw their folly and misfortune, but could not, in the distraction they were in, so soon redress it. The city was in actual process of being **sacked**, the enemy putting the men to the sword, demolishing the fortifications, and dragging the women and children, with lamentable shrieks and cries, prisoners into the castle. The commanders, giving all for lost, could give no present order, nor have their men to serve them against their enemies, that came hand over head on every side amongst them.

The city being thus miserably in **garboil**, and the Acradina also in great hazard of taking, in the which they put all their hope and confidence to rise again, every man thought then with himself that Dion must be sent for; but yet no man moved it notwithstanding, being ashamed of their unthankfulness and overgreat folly they had committed in driving him away. Yet necessity enforcing them unto it, there were certain of the horsemen and of their confederates that cried they must send for Dion, and the Peloponnesians his soldiers, which were with him in the territory of the Leontines.

[Omission for length: Representatives were sent to Dion, who made a speech and thereby gained support for the idea of "liberating" Syracuse.]

So when all was quiet, Dion willed them forthwith to go and prepare themselves, and that they should be there ready armed after supper, determining the very same night to go to aid Syracuse.

Part Two

But now at Syracuse, while daylight lasted, Dionysius' soldiers and captains did all the mischief and villainy they could in the city; and when night came, they retired again into their castle, having lost very few of their men. Then the **seditious governors** of the Syracusans took heart again unto them, hoping that the enemies would be contented with that they had done: and therefore began anew to persuade the citizens to **let Dion alone**, and not to receive him with his mercenary soldiers if they came to aid him; advising them not to yield, as inferior to them in point of honour and courage, but to save their city and defend their liberties and properties themselves.

So other ambassadors were sent again unto Dion, some from the captains and governors of the city, to stay them that they should not come; but others also from the horsemen, and the noble citizens his friends, to hasten his journey. Whereupon by reason of this variance, **Dion marched very softly at his ease**.

Part Three

Now by night, Dion's enemies within the city got to the gates, and kept them that Dion should not come in.

Nypsius, on the other side, made a sally out of the castle with his mercenary soldiers, being better appointed and a greater number of them than before; and with them he straight plucked down all the wall which they had built before the castle, and ran and **sacked the city** *[omission for content]*. For, because Dionysius saw that he was brought to a **strait and desperate case**, he bore such **mortal malice** against the Syracusans, that if there was no remedy but that he must needs forego his tyranny, he determined to bury it with the utter destruction and desolation of their city. And therefore, to prevent Dion's aid, and to make a quick dispatch to destroy all, they came with burning torches in their hands, and did set fire of all things they could come to: and further off, they fired their darts and arrows, and bestowed them in every place of the city. So, they that fled for the fire, were met withal, and slain in the streets by the soldiers, and others also that ran into their houses, were driven out again by force of fire. For there were a number of houses that were afire, and fell down upon them that went and came.

This misery was the chiefest cause why all the Syracusans agreed together to set open the gates unto Dion. For when Dion heard, by the way, that Dionysius' soldiers were gone again into the castle, he made no great haste to march forward; but when day was broken, there came certain horsemen from Syracuse unto Dion, who brought him news that the enemies had once again taken the city. Then also came others of his enemies unto him, and prayed him to make haste. The pressure increasing, Heracleides sent his brother, and after him his uncle, Theodotes, to beg him to help them; for that now they were not able to resist any longer; he himself was wounded, and the greatest part of the city either in ruins or in flames.

When this news came to Dion, he was yet about **sixty furlongs** from the city. So he told his mercenary soldiers the danger the town was in, and having encouraged them, he led them no more fair and softly, but running towards the city, and meeting messengers upon messengers entreating them to make haste. By this means, the soldiers marching with wonderful speed and goodwill together, he entered the gates of the city at a place called Hecatompedon.

First of all, he sent the lightest-armed men he had against the enemies, to the end that, the Syracusans seeing them, they might take a good heart again to themselves; whilst he himself in the meantime did set all the other heavy-armed soldiers and citizens that came to join with him, in battle array, and did cast them into divers squadrons of greater length than breadth, and appointed them that should have the leading of them, to the end that setting upon the enemies in divers places together, they should put them in the greater fear and terror.

When he had set all things in this order, and had made his prayers unto the gods, and that they saw him marching through the city against their enemies, then there rose such a common noise and rejoicing, and great shout of the soldiers, mingled with vows, prayers, and persuasions of all the Syracusans, that they called Dion their god and saviour, and the mercenary soldiers their brethren and fellow citizens. Furthermore, there was not a Syracusan that so much regarded his own life and person, but he seemed to be more afraid of the loss of Dion only, than of all the rest. For they saw him the foremost man running through the danger of the fire, treading in blood, and upon dead bodies that lay slain in the midst of the streets.

Now indeed to charge the enemies, it was a marvellous dangerous enterprise: for they were like mad beasts, and stood beside in battle array along the wall which they had overthrown, in a very dangerous place, and hard to win. Howbeit the danger of the fire did most of all trouble and amaze the strangers, and did stop their way. For, on which side soever they turned them, the houses round about them were all of a fire, and they were driven to march over the burnt timber of the houses, and to run in great danger of the walls of the house sides that fell on them, and to pass through the thick smoke mingled with dust, and beside, to keep their ranks with great difficulty.

And when they came to assail the enemies, they could not come to fight hand to hand, but a few of them in number, because of the straitness of the place: howbeit the Syracusans with force of cries and shouts did so animate and encourage their men, that at length they drove Nypsius and his men to forsake the place. The most part of them got into the castle, being very near unto them: the other that could not get in in time, fled straggling up and down, whom the Grecian soldiers slew, chasing of them.

The extremity of the time did not presently suffer the conquerors to reap the fruit of their victory, neither the joys and embracings meet for so great an exploit. For the Syracusans went every man home to his own house, to quench the fire, the which could scarcely be put out all the night.

Narration and Discussion

Why was it so difficult for Dion's soldiers to get through the city to the castle? Why was their victory a bittersweet one?

It has been said previously that Dion was not a young man anymore, and not in top physical shape; did this seem to affect his leadership? How did others view him? Show examples from the passage.

Creative narration: Use the model you built to narrate this lesson.

Lesson Eleven

Introduction

The siege continued until, at last, Dion reached an agreement with Apollocrates, the son of Dionysius. However, the storm clouds were gathering for a final showdown with Heracleides.

Vocabulary

popular haranguers: North calls them the "seditious flatterers of the people"; those who had led the anti-government group

yield them to the desires…: let the soldiers treat them as they wished

ambitious affectation of popularity: the threat of democracy

clemency: mercy

meeter: better, fairer

line of palisade: wall made of stakes

engage: fight

inconsiderable: small, slight

at a jar: at odds, squabbling

redeem their credit: restore their honour

seven hundred furlongs: 87.5 miles (140.8 km)

tack: change course by heading a boat into the wind

head: lead the Sicilian force

amulet: lucky charm

being himself a citizen of Sparta: During Dion's time in Greece, he had been made an honourary Spartan.

embarked: gone on board the ship

thralldom: slavery

People

Pharax: also called **Pharacidas**; a Spartan admiral

Gaesylus: a Spartan general

Historic Occasions

354 B.C.: Apollocrates' departure left Syracuse in Dion's hands

On the Map

Agrigentum: Agrigentum (Agrigento) is on the south coast of Sicily.

Reading

Part One

When day broke, not one of the **popular haranguers** dared stay in the city, but all of them, knowing their own guilt, by their flight confessed it, and secured their lives.

Heracleides and Theodotes came together of their own goodwill to yield themselves unto Dion, confessing that they had done him wrong, and humbly praying him to show himself better unto them than they had showed themselves unto him: and that it was more honourable for him, being every way unmatchable for his virtues, to show himself more noble to conquer his anger, than his unthankful enemies had done: who, contending with him before in virtue, did now confess themselves to be far inferior unto him. Though they thus humbly addressed him, his friends advised him not to pardon these wicked men, who did malice and envy his honour; but to **yield them to the desires of his soldiers**, and utterly root out of the commonwealth the **ambitious affectation of popularity**, which was as dangerous and great a plague to a city as the tyranny. Dion endeavoured to satisfy them, telling them that:

> "other generals exercised and trained themselves for the most part in the practices of war and arms; but that he had long studied in the Academy how to conquer anger, and not let emulation and envy conquer him; that to do this it is not sufficient that a man be obliging and kind to his friends, and those that have deserved well of him, but, rather, gentle and ready to forgive in the case of those who do wrong; that he wished to let the world see that he valued not himself so much upon excelling Heracleides in ability and conduct, as he did in outdoing him in justice and **clemency**; for therein chiefly consisted excellency, since no man else in wars can challenge power and government, but fortune, that ruleth most. 'And though Heracleides,' said he, 'through envy hath done like a wicked man, must Dion therefore through anger blemish his virtue? Indeed by man's law it is thought **meeter**, to revenge an injury offered, than to do an injury; but nature showeth that they both proceed of the same deficiency and weakness. Now, though it be a hard thing to change and alter the evil disposition of a man, after he is once nurtured in villainy, yet is not man of so wild and brutish a nature that his wickedness may not be overcome by kindness, and altered by repeated obligations."

Dion, making use of these arguments, pardoned and dismissed Heracleides and Theodotes.

Part Two

And now, resolving to repair the blockade about the castle, he commanded all the Syracusans to cut each man a stake and bring it to the works; and then, dismissing them to refresh themselves and take their rest, he employed his own men all night, and by morning had finished his **line of palisade**; so that both the enemy and the citizens wondered, when day returned, to see the work so far advanced in so short a time. Burying, therefore, the dead, and redeeming the prisoners, who were near two thousand, he called a public assembly, where Heracleides made a motion that Dion should be declared general of Syracuse, with absolute power and authority, both by sea and land.

The chiefest men of the city liked very well of it, and would have had the people to have passed it. But the mob of sailors and tradespeople would not yield that Heracleides should lose his command of the navy: believing him, if otherwise an ill man, at any rate to be more citizen-like than Dion, and readier to comply with the people. Dion, therefore, submitted to them in this, and consented that Heracleides should continue as admiral.

But when they began to press the project of the redistribution of lands and houses, he not only opposed it, but repealed all the votes they had formerly made upon that account, which angered them.

Wherefore Heracleides, remaining at Messina, began thenceforth to enter into new practices again, and to flatter the soldiers and seafaring men he had brought thither with him, and to stir them up to rebel against Dion, saying that he (Dion) would make himself tyrant; and himself in the meantime secretly practised with Dionysius, by means of a Spartan called **Pharax**. The noblest men of the Syracusans mistrusted it, and thereupon there fell out great mutiny in their camp; and the city was in great distress and want of provisions. Dion now knew not what course to take, being also blamed by all his friends for having thus fortified against himself such a malicious and wicked person as Heracleides was.

Part Three

Pharax at this time lay encamped at Neapolis, in the territory of **Agrigentum**. Dion, therefore, led out the Syracusans, but with an intent not to **engage** him till he saw a fit opportunity. But Heracleides and his seamen exclaimed against him, that he had delayed fighting on purpose that he might the longer continue his command; so that, much against his will, he was forced to an engagement and was beaten; his loss, however, being **inconsiderable**, happened rather because his men were **at a jar** among themselves, by reason of their faction and division, than otherwise. He rallied his men, and, having put them in good order and encouraged them to **redeem their credit**, resolved upon a second battle. But in the evening, he received advice that Heracleides with his fleet was on his way to Syracuse, with the purpose to possess himself of the city and keep him and his army out. Instantly, therefore, taking with him some of the strongest and most active of his men, he rode off in the dark, and about nine the next morning was at the gates, having ridden **seven hundred furlongs** that night.

Part Four

Heracleides strove to make all the speed he could; yet, coming too late, he **tacked** and stood out again to sea; and, being unresolved what course to steer, accidentally he met **Gaesylus** the Spartan, who told him he was come from Lacedaemon to **head** the Sicilians, as Gylippus had formerly done. Heracleides was only too glad to get hold of him, and fastening him as it might be a sort of **amulet** to himself, he showed him to the confederates, and sent a herald to Syracuse to summon them to accept the Spartan general.

Dion made answer that the Syracusans had governors enough, and though that their affairs did of necessity require a Lacedaemonian captain, yet that himself was he, **being himself a citizen of Sparta**. Then Gaesylus perceiving he could not obtain to be general, he went unto Syracuse, and came to Dion, and there made Heracleides and him friends again, by the great and solemn oaths he made, and because Gaesylus also swore, that he himself would be revenged of him for Dion's sake, and punish Heracleides, if ever after he did once more conspire against him.

Part Five

After that, the Syracusans broke up their navy, because it did them then no service, and was besides a great charge to keep it, and, further, it did also breed sedition and trouble amongst their governors; and so they pressed on the siege, and built up the wall again which the enemies had overthrown.

Then Apollocrates (Dionysius' son) seeing no aid to come to him from any part, and that victuals failed them, and further, that the soldiers began to mutiny, being unable to keep them, he agreed with Dion to deliver up the castle into his hands, with all the armour and munition in it: and so he took his mother and his sisters, and put them aboard upon five galleys, with the which he went unto his father, Dion seeing him safely out; and scarce a man in all the city not being there to behold the sight, as indeed they called even on those that were not present, out of pity, that they could not be there to see this happy day and the sun shining on a free Syracuse. If until this present day they do reckon the fleeing of Dionysius for one of the rarest examples of Fortune's change, as one of the greatest and notablest thing that ever was, what joy think we had they that drove him out; and what pleasure had they with themselves, that with the least means that could be possible, did destroy the greatest tyranny in the world?

So when Apollocrates was **embarked**, and Dion was entered into the castle, the women within the castle would not tarry till he came into the house, but went to meet him at the gates, Aristomache leading Dion's son by the hand, and Arete following her, weeping, being very fearful how she should call and salute her husband, after living with another man. Dion first spoke to his sister, and afterwards to his son: and then Aristomache, offering him Arete, said unto him:

> "Since thy banishment, O Dion, we have led a miserable and captive life: but now that thou art returned home with victory, thou hast rid us out of care and **thralldom**, and hast also made us again bold to lift up our heads, saving her here, whom I, wretched creature, was compelled to see another's while you were yet alive. Now then, since Fortune hath made thee lord of us all, what judgment givest thou of this compulsion? How wilt thou have her to

> salute thee, as her uncle, or husband?"

As Aristomache spoke these words, the water stood in Dion's eyes: so he gently and lovingly taking his wife Arete by the hand, he gave her his son, and willed her to go home to his house where he then remained, and so delivered the castle to the Syracusans.

[omission for length]

Narration and Discussion

What surprised the Syracusans most when they saw the repaired blockade? How might those inside the castle have reacted?

Dion said, "Though it be a hard thing to change and alter the evil disposition of a man, after he is once nurtured in villainy, yet is not man of so wild and brutish a nature that his wickedness may not be overcome by kindness..." Do you agree?

For further thought: Christian teaching says that we should overcome anger with love and forgiveness. But is there a time when it is not wise to show mercy too quickly? Is there a difference between forgiving wrongs, and excusing sin or allowing it to continue?

Creative narration #1: Use the model you built to narrate this lesson. (This will be the last time it is needed.)

Creative narration #2: Imagine that you are a poet living in Syracuse, and write something to commemorate the occasion.

Lesson Twelve and Examination Questions

Introduction

In a passage omitted for length, Plutarch describes Dion's activities and status at this time: he busied himself rewarding those who had served or helped to liberate Syracuse, but he seemed to want little material reward for himself. According to Plutarch, what he did seem to care about was the good opinion of the Academy philosophers in Athens, who, he was sure, were watching him to see how he handled his "prosperous success and victory."

Now that the tyranny was ended, the burning question in Syracuse was, what kind of a government should replace it, and who would lead it? Dion wanted to set up a ruling council of nobles, and he asked the rulers of Corinth for help in implementing it.

However, he was opposed, as always, by Heracleides, and he finally decided that this longtime enemy must be disposed of. What the Academy made of that, we are not told. But even without Heracleides, Dion's enemies, and even his friends, continued to plot against him.

Vocabulary

Celebration of the Mysteries: an Athenian religious ritual

gallantry: courageous behaviour

twenty talents: a huge amount of money

inveigle: persuade

feign: pretend

consort with people: to spend time in their company

apparition: ghost, spirit

gallery: a room in a building formed partly of columns (a **colonnade**)

man's estate: adulthood

displeasure and pet: fit of sulks, tantrum

fidelity: loyalty, faithfulness

dispatch: kill

great with child: about to have a baby

hemlock: a poisonous plant

People

Callippus: first mentioned in **Lesson Four**

Historic Occasions

354 B.C.: Death of Heracleides

354 B.C.: Death of Dion

348/347 B.C.: Death of Plato

347/346 B.C.: Dionysius II returned to Syracuse

344 B.C.: Syracuse appealed to Corinth for aid; Timoleon invaded Syracuse (see the *Life of Timoleon*); Dionysius surrendered

343 B.C.: Death of Dionysius II in Corinth

Reading

Part One

[See the Introduction for a synopsis of the omitted passage. Dion, facing political opposition from Heracleides, and believing that "in all ways he was a turbulent, fickle, and factious man," arranged to have him murdered. Dion apparently did not try to keep his part in this a secret, and he explained publicly that it was necessary to end the continued friction.]

Dion had a friend called **Callippus**, an Athenian, who, Plato says, first made acquaintance and afterwards obtained familiarity with him, not from any connection with his philosophic studies, but on occasions afforded by the **Celebration of the Mysteries**, and in the way of ordinary society. This man went with him in all his military service, and was in great honour and esteem; being the first of his friends who marched by his side into Syracuse, wearing a garland upon his head, having behaved himself very well in all the battles, and made himself remarkable for his **gallantry**.

This Callippus, seeing that Dion's best and chiefest friends were all slain in this war, and that Heracleides also was dead; that the people of Syracuse were without a leader; and besides, that the soldiers which were with Dion did love him better than any other man: he became the unfaithfullest man and the veriest villain of all others, hoping that, as his reward for the ruin of his friend and benefactor, he should undoubtedly come to have the whole government of all Sicily; and some report that he had taken a bribe of his enemies of **twenty talents** to destroy Dion. He **inveigled** and engaged several of the soldiers in a conspiracy against him, taking this cunning and wicked occasion for his plot. He daily informed Dion of what he heard or what he **feigned** the soldiers said against him; whereby he gained that credit and confidence, that he was allowed by Dion to **consort** privately with whom he would, and talk freely against him in any company: to the end he might thereby understand the better whether any of the soldiers were angry with him, or wished his death. By this means, Callippus straight found out those that held a grudge against Dion, and that were already corrupted, whom he drew to his conspiracy. And if any man unwilling to give ear unto him went and told Dion that Callippus would have enticed him to conspire against him: Dion was not angry with him for it, thinking that he did but as he had commanded him to do.

While this conspiracy was afoot, a strange and dreadful **apparition** was seen by Dion. As he sat one evening in a **gallery** in his house, alone and thoughtful, hearing a sudden noise, he turned about, and saw at the end of the **colonnade**, by clear daylight, a tall woman, in her countenance and garb like one of the Furies shown in plays, with a broom in her hand, sweeping the floor. This vision so amazed and affrighted him that he sent for his friends, and told them what a sight he had seen: and prayed them to tarry with him all night, being as it were a man beside himself, fearing lest the spirit would come to him again if they left him alone. He saw it no more.

But a few days after, his only son, being almost grown up to **man's estate**, upon some **displeasure and pet** he had taken upon a childish and frivolous occasion, threw himself headlong from the top of the house and broke his neck. While Dion was under this affliction, Callippus drove on his conspiracy, and spread a rumour among the Syracusans that Dion, being now childless, was resolved to send for Dionysius' son, Apollocrates, who was his wife's nephew and sister's grandson, and make him his heir and successor.

By this time, Dion and his wife and sister began to suspect what was doing, and from all hands information came to them of the plot. Dion being troubled, it is probable, for Heracleides' murder, which was like to be a blot and stain upon his life and actions, in continual weariness and vexation, he had rather die a thousand deaths, and to offer his throat to be cut to any that would, rather than live not only in fear of his enemies but suspicion of his friends.

But Callippus, seeing the women very inquisitive to search to the bottom of the business, took alarm, and came to them, utterly denying it with tears in his eyes, and offering to give them whatever assurances of his **fidelity** they desired. They required that he should take the Great Oath *[a religious ritual; details omitted for length]*.

Part Two

[But] as Dion was set in his chamber talking with his friends, where there were many beds to sit on, some of the conspirators compassed the house round about; others came to the doors and windows of his chamber; and they that should do the deed to **dispatch** him, which were the Zacynthian soldiers, came into his chamber in their coats without any sword. But when they were come in, they that were without did shut the doors after them, and locked them in, lest any man should come out: and they that were within, fell upon Dion, and thought to have strangled him. But when they saw they could not, they called for a sword. Never a man that was within dared open the doors, though there were many with Dion. For they thought every man to save their own lives, by suffering him to be killed, and therefore dared not come to help him.

So the murderers tarried a long time within, and did nothing. At length there was one Lycon, a Syracusan, that gave one of these Zacynthian soldiers a dagger in at the window, and thus, like a victim at a sacrifice, this long time in their power and trembling for the blow, they killed him. They hurried his sister, and wife, **great with child**, into prison, and there the poor lady was pitifully brought to bed of a goodly boy: which, by the consent of the keepers, they (the women) intended to bring up.

Their keepers that had the charge of them, were contented to let them do it, because Callippus began then a little to grow to some trouble. For at the first, after he had slain Dion, he bore all the whole sway for a time, and kept the city of Syracuse in his hands: and wrote unto Athens, the which next unto the immortal gods he was most afraid of, having defiled his hands in so damnable a treason. And therefore, in my opinion, it was not evil spoken, that Athens is a city of all other that bringeth forth the best men when they give themselves to goodness, and the wickedest people also, when they do dispose themselves to evil: as their country also produces the most delicious honey and the most deadly **hemlock**.

Callippus, however, did not long continue to scandalize Fortune and upbraid the gods with his prosperity, as though they connived at and bore with the wretched man while he purchased riches and power by heinous impieties; but he quickly received the punishment he deserved.

[Omission for length: the further adventures and death of Callippus, and the murder of Dion's family members.]

Narration and Discussion

What led to Dion's downfall? Were there errors that, if avoided, could have changed the end of this story?

Plutarch says that Dion would rather "offer his throat to be cut to any that would, rather than live not only in fear of his enemies but suspicion of his friends." Where had Dion previously seen an example of such a life?

How do you think that Callippus was able to bribe the mercenary soldiers to participate in the assassination? Do you think they trusted Dion less after the death of Heracleides, or was it simply the power of a bribe? (Here are some Scriptures describing what bribes can do: Deuteronomy 16:19, Proverbs 17:23, Micah 7:3.)

For older students: In either written or oral format, discuss the positive and negative aspects of a government where everyone has a voice, vs. one where a small group of people (such as the nobles) make most of the decisions.

Examination Questions

Younger Students:

1. Describe a) the early life of Dionysius II, and b) how he was affected by his time with Plato.

   OR

2. Describe the early life of Dion, and how he came to be so important in Syracuse.

Older Students:

1. Write a conversation between two Syracusans, one who thinks Dion is a valuable asset and a good person to have around, and another who wishes they could rid themselves of him.

2. (High school) Plato named four key virtues: prudence, fortitude, temperance (moderation and self-control), and justice. How did Dion's life reflect these?

Bibliography

Plutarch's Lives of the Noble Greeks and Romans. Englished by Sir Thomas North. With an introduction by George Wyndham. London: Dent, 1894. (Phocion, Furius Camillus, Dion)

Plutarch's Lives: The Dryden Plutarch. Revised by Arthur Hugh Clough. London: J.M. Dent, 1910. (Phocion, Camillus, Dion)

About the Author

Anne E. White (www.annewrites.ca) has shared her knowledge of Charlotte Mason's methods through magazine columns, online writing, and conference workshops. She is an Advisory member of AmblesideOnline and the author of *Minds More Awake: The Vision of Charlotte Mason* and *Honest, Simple Souls: An Advent Meditation with Charlotte Mason*, as well as other books in The Plutarch Project series.

Made in the USA
Monee, IL
06 January 2024